Caxton: Paris and Vienne

EARLY ENGLISH TEXT SOCIETY
Original Series, No. 234

hys fader / & that other to hys
felawe Edwarde / Of whyche the
letter to hys fader sayd in thys
manere /

Ryght dere & honourable
ſyr and fader playſe it
you to wete þat I am
moche ſorowful and heuy of my
cruel aduenture / and alſo I en
dure grete heuynes / ſorowe and
afflyctyon / doubtyng þat for
me ye haue ſuffred grete payne
and trybulacyon / and I late
you wete that I am at gence / &
dwelle in a lodgyng a ſtone &
poſed fro al joyes and conſola
cyons mondayne / For myn en
tendement is to ſerue god and
our lady fro hens forth / & pur
poſe that ye ſhal ſee me no more /
for I wyl departe & goo thurgh
the worlde to ſeche holy pylgry
mages / And yf by aduenture I
ſhal dye tofore that ye ſhal ſee
me / I praye you that it may
playſe you that I dye not in
your euyl wylle / But humbly by
ſeche you that it playſe yon to
pardonne me / and to gyue to me
your benedyctyon / Alſo dere ſyr
and fader I praye you & ſupplye
that my dere brother and felowe
Edwarde ye wyl take in my
name and place / and that he
be recommaunded as your ſone
in ſtede of me / as wel in your
ſeruyage as in other thynges /
and the grace of the holy ghoſt
be wyth you / Recommaunde me

to my moder & c / And the letter
of Edward ſayd thus /

Dere and ſpecyal brother
and ſynguler frende ed
warde the peryl of paris
and of hys aduenture is your
ſcribed of alle euyl and cruel
fortune / I commaunde me to you
as moche as I may ſay or thynk
Neuertheles lyke as we haue
ben accuſtomed to wryte letters
of loue and of chyualrye / Now
I muſt wryte letters anguyſ
ſhous of ſorowe and of euyl
fortune / for alas I am Unſa py
al allone in a ſtrange contre / &
exyled fro al joyes and fro alle
playſyr / and out of al worldly
playſaunce thynkyng nyght &
day on the bele Uyenne / the why
che I thynke that for me hath ſuf
fred mortal ſorowe / and I ſay
to you that yf I knewe that for
me ſhe ſuffred payne and ſorowe
I ſhold be in deſpayr / for I am
worthy for to be punyſſhed cru
elly for that fayte & none other
wherfore I praye god and alle
hys ſayntes that ſhe may be
kepte from al euyl / and gyue
hyr grace to proſpere in al good
and honour lyke as ſhe is wor
thy and myn herte deſyreth /
¶ My dere broder & felowe the
mooſt dere thynges that I loue
in thys worlde is fyrſt the fayr
and ſwete Uyenne / & next you
to whom I praye you yf it may

William Caxton: *Paris and Vienne* [sig. c v^r]
(reduced)

Paris and Vienne

Translated from the French and printed
by William Caxton

EDITED BY

MacEDWARD LEACH

Published for
THE EARLY ENGLISH TEXT SOCIETY
by
OXFORD UNIVERSITY PRESS
LONDON NEW YORK TORONTO

OXFORD

Great Clarendon Street, Oxford OX2 6DP
United Kingdom

Oxford University Press is a department of the University of Oxford.
It furthers the University's objective of excellence in research, scholarship,
and education by publishing worldwide. Oxford is a registered trade mark of
Oxford University Press in the UK and in certain other countries

© The Early English Text Society 1957

The moral rights of the authors have been asserted

Database right Oxford University Press (maker)

First Edition published in 1957 (for 1951)
Reprinted 1970

All rights reserved. No part of this publication may be reproduced,
stored in a retrieval system, or transmitted, in any form or by any means,
without the prior permission in writing of Oxford University Press,
or as expressly permitted by law, or under terms agreed with the appropriate
reprographics rights organization. Enquiries concerning reproduction
outside the scope of the above should be sent to the Rights Department,
Oxford University Press, at the address above

You must not circulate this book in any other form
and you must impose this same condition on any acquirer

Published in the United States of America by Oxford University Press
198 Madison Avenue, New York, NY 10016, United States of America

British Library Cataloguing in Publication Data
Data available

Library of Congress Cataloging in Publication Data
Data available

Original Series, 234

ISBN 978-0-19-722234-8

PREFACE

Towards the end of the Middle Ages a new kind of story appeared in western Europe. These new stories show both a reaction against earlier romance and a reflection of new culture patterns that were replacing those of the Middle Ages. They are more realistic, more local, more circumstantial in detail, and closer to actual life. They are of the here and now rather than of the far away and long ago. Most of them are in prose. Often psychological motivation integrates character and action. *Paris and Vienne* is one of the most charming of these stories.

The difference between these and earlier romance is admirably put by Pierre de la Cypede, one of the translators of *Paris and Vienne*, in his preface to the early French version. He remarked that he found the old stories, such as those of Launcelot, Tristan, Florimond, and Guy of Warwick, 'very impossible to believe'; accordingly he turned, he said, to *Paris and Vienne* because 'the matter is reasonable and tolerably credible and the story is pleasing'. All of which says that the old stories are no longer reasonable or credible and perhaps not so pleasing.

Paris and Vienne was brought into English in 1485 by William Caxton, who translated it from French and printed it. It was re-issued by another press in 1492, reprinted by the Caxton press in 1502, and again by a third press in 1510. Only one complete copy of the Caxton 1485 printing has survived. It is now in the British Museum. In 1868 it was transcribed and edited by W. C. Hazlitt for the Roxburghe Club. The Hazlitt edition contains an accurate text, but its editorial apparatus is meagre and the book has long been out of print. I have endeavoured in this edition to provide a letter-perfect transcription of the Caxton text, with adequate introduction, notes, and glossary.

I am indebted to the authorities of the British Museum, of the Bibliothèque Nationale, of the Bodleian, and of the

Cleveland Public Library for permission to microfilm and print material under their jurisdiction. The Staff of the University of Pennsylvania has been very helpful in securing books and microfilms. I wish to thank the Committee on Faculty Research of the University of Pennsylvania for a grant to help pay for clerical aid. To R. W. Burchfield, Hon. Secretary of the Early English Text Society, I am very grateful for constant and invaluable assistance. Finally, I wish to acknowledge the debt I owe to my wife, Nancy Leach, for continual help and especially for transcribing texts and tracking down references.

MACEDWARD LEACH

Philadelphia
November 22, 1955

CONTENTS

William Caxton: *Paris and Vienne* [sig. c v^r]   *Frontispiece*

PREFACE   v

INTRODUCTION   ix
   The Different Versions of the Story
   The Origin and Date of the Story
   Caxton and the Story in French
   Caxton as Translator

TEXT   1

NOTES   79

GLOSSARY   107

INTRODUCTION

The Different Versions of the Story

Paris and Vienne occurs in two versions widely dispersed over Europe. The first of these versions, the older, is found in six important manuscripts in French; the second version occurs in one French and several Italian manuscripts and in many early printed texts in English, Flemish, Spanish, Catalan, German, Italian, Russian, Swedish, and Latin.

The French manuscripts of Version I are as follows:

(1) A fragment of three pages from two manuscripts in the Library of Carpentras (Number 1792, Folio 285). One page in a late-fifteenth-century or early-sixteenth-century hand begins the romance at 1r with the prologue of Pierre de la Cypede. It begins: '[B]arlan qui mot fu saige . . .' The prologue ends at the top of 1v: 'je suis de saint piere jay prins le non de la cypede pour sour non et fut en commance a escripre cest libre lan de grace mil (CCCC) XXXII le tiers jour del moys de septembre et pour moy Inart beyssan traylatie M (CCCC) XXXVIII a XVII du moys de februer'. 2r and 2v are mere scraps, so damaged that not a sentence is preserved intact; 3r and 3v are likewise badly damaged. Since these two pages are in a different hand from that of 1, and since the paper is different, we apparently have fragments of two different manuscripts. Folios 2 and 3 seem to tell the episode of the serenade, 3/16 ff. of the Caxton text.[1]

(2) B.N. Fr. 1480. (1452). 201 folio pages. Originally in the library of the Marquis de Cangé. It begins with the usual prologue: 'Alain qui moult fu saige . . .' The text ends: 'a la gloyre de paradis a laquelle gloyre puissons tous pervenir. Amen.' The colophon ends: 'cest liure fust acheue le XXIXe iour de nouembre lan mil CCCC cinquante et deux'. In another

---

[1] Duhamel et Liabastres *Catalogue général des manuscrits des bibliothèques publiques de France* (Paris 1899) XXXV (Carpentras II) 336; C. Chabaneau 'Sur quelques manuscrits provençaux perdus ou égarés' *Revue des langues romanes* Series III Vol. XII (1884) 211–13; Robert Kaltenbacher 'Der altfranzösische Roman Paris et Vienne' *Romanische Forschungen* XV (1904) 338 and 630–2.

x *Introduction*

hand is the note 'Roman de Paris et Vienne (fille de Godefroy de Lanson Dauphin de Vienne) traduit en 1443 du Prouençal qui l'auoit esté du Catalan'.[1]

(3) B.N. Fr. 1464 (Anc. 7544[2]). 129 folio pages. The date given in the prologue is 1443. The prologue begins: 'Alain qui moult fut saige...' The text ends: '... en la gloire de paradis a laquelle puissions nous tous parvenire Amen Explicit le liure de Paris et de Vienne'.[2]

(4) B.N. Fr. 1479. (1459). 98 folio pages. The inside cover bears the sentence: 'Traicte de Godefroy dalenson et de Paris son gendre compose par Pierre de la Suppade de la ville de marseille en 1432 et ecrit par Guillaume le Moign en 1459...' The story opens with the usual prologue which here ends: 'par la main de guillem le moign le XVIe iour du moys de ianuier mil IIIILIX'.[3]

(5) Bibliothèque de l'Arsenal 3000. 107 folio pages. This manuscript like B.N. 1480 and B.N. 1464 gives the date at the end of the prologue as December 6, 1443.[4]

(6) Bibliothèque Royale Brussels 9632-3. 136 folio pages. The prologue gives the date as 'lan de grace mil IIIᶜ XXXII le tiers jour de moys de septembre'.[5]

These six manuscripts are all closely related. They contain the oldest version of the story. Kaltenbacher edited all of them, using B.N.1480 as his basic text.[6]

The texts belonging to Version II that are important to the present study are the following:

(1) B.N. Fr. 20044. 58 folios, 4º. This manuscript is in a difficult fifteenth-century hand; in many places the letters are so run together and so imperfectly made that they are impossible to decipher. Mutilations—the most serious is on f. 28 —and blots add further to the difficulties. One leaf after f. 50 is missing. The prologue always found in Version I

[1] Bibliothèque nationale *Catalogue des manuscrits français*, Ancien fonds (Paris 1868) I 234-5; Kaltenbacher *op. cit.* 339.
[2] Bibliothèque nationale *op. cit.* 233; Kaltenbacher *op. cit.* 339.
[3] Bibliothèque nationale *op. cit.* 234; Kaltenbacher *op. cit.* 339.
[4] Henry Martin *Catalogue des manuscrits de la bibliothèque de l'Arsenal* (Paris 1887) III 188; Kaltenbacher *op. cit.* 338.
[5] F. J. F. Marchal *Catalogue des manuscrits de la bibliothèque royale des ducs de Bourgogne* (Brussels 1842) I 193; Kaltenbacher *op. cit.* 340.
[6] *op. cit.* 321-688.

is not present here; the text begins in large letters: 'Au temps du roy' which extend across the whole page, and then proceeds in small closely written cursive 'charles roy de france ...' It ends: '... en la gloire de paradis Amen' and then in a following line set in with deep indentation: 'Scriptor qui scripsit cum xpo viuere possit'. There is no indication of date, or translator, or scribe.[1]

(2) The printed text of Gherard Leeu, Antwerp, 1487. This is the earliest known printed text of the story in French. It is a book of 39 pages printed in double columns, with numerous wood-cuts and ornamental capitals. Each chapter begins with a heading. It lacks a title-page, but the blank page opposite the beginning carries the prologue as found in B.N. 1480 and the four lines of verse also found at the end of 1480:

> Dieu doint aux trespasses sa gloyre
> Et aux viuans force et victoyre
> Que ilz la puissent conquerir
> Cy veulh lystoyre finir.

Then comes the statement: 'iay extrait ce qui precede dun ancien manuscrit en prose qui mapartient'. The text begins with the heading: 'Cy commence listoire du tresuaillant cheualier paris ...' It ends: 'cy finist listoire du vaillant et noble cheualier paris. Et de la belle Vienne fille du daulphin de Viennois. Emprientee en Anuers par moy Gherard leeu lan mil cccc.lxxxvii. le xve iour du mois de may'.

The only known copy of Leeu's book is in the Bibliothèque Nationale, old listing y/2 222.[2]

(3) The text of William Caxton, translated by Caxton from French and printed by him at Westminster, December 19, 1485. 35 pages. The type is Caxton 4*. The pages are set double column, 39 lines to the column. Collation: a, b, and c are 4^{ns}; d and e 3^{ns}. Each section begins with a heading a sentence or two long and preceded by a paragraph mark (¶). Woodcut

---

[1] L. Auvray et H. Omont *Catalogue des manuscrits de la Bibliothèque Nationale. Ancien Saint-Germain Français* (Paris 1900) III 471; Kaltenbacher *op. cit.* 340–1.

[2] Jacques-Charles Brunet *Manuel du libraire et de l'amateur de livres* (Paris 1863) IV 371; Jean Graesse *Trésor de livres rares et précieux* ... (Dresden 1859–69) V 134–5; Kaltenbacher *op. cit.* 341.

capitals are used at the beginning of each large section of the story. The book has no title-page and no prologue. The text begins immediately at the top of a j^r without a title but with a long heading setting forth the theme of the story. It ends with a rather long colophon, giving the date of printing and translation. The only known copy is in the British Museum.[1]

The two versions of the story are essentially the same in outline; they are, however, quite different in details. Version I is much more circumstantial, filling in every scene with much detail and with descriptive background. It is more than twice the length of Version II. Characteristic of these differences are the following passages. The first is from B.N. Fr. 1464, ff. 103–4, representing Version I, and the second from B.N. Fr. 20044, f. 30^r, and from Gherard Leeu's print of 1487, both representing Version II. The same passage is given from Caxton's translation for comparison.

Puis elle tira ung petit dyament, qu'elle portoit en son doy, et dist a Paris: 'Messire Paris, vees cy cest annel que je vous donne en nom de mariage, si vous prye que le veulhes bien garder, car quant vous le verres, ce sera occasion qu'il vous doye de moy souvenir. Si vous supplie que pour chouse que advenir vous puisse, ne me veulhes oblier. Or vous en alles, et je prye au benoist filz de Dieu qu'il vous veulhe conduire et vostre corps garder de villanye et nous doint revoer ainsi comme nous desirons.' Paris prist l'annel mes il ne peust ung tout seul mot dire ne respondre, car le cuer luy vint si groux, que les lermes luy vindrent aux yeulx a grant foyson. Si hurta son cheval des esperons et s'en va ainsi comme celuy qui est enraige de dueil et de courroux. Et Vienne luy cria a haulte voys: 'Paris, je vous requier que il vuos soveigne tousjours de moy, quar ainsi sera il a moy de vous.'

Atant chevaucha Paris tout seul qu'il vint a la riviere. Si la trova molt grosse et courrant mes comme celuy qui avoit perdu sens et memoire, se fourra dedans comme forcene; et la rivyere le commenca a porter contre val, mes ainsi comme fortune le vouloit pour la volunte de Dieu, ou pour la force du cheval, qui molt bon estoit,

---

[1] William Blades *The Biography and Typography of William Caxton* (London 1882) pp. 308–10; Seymour de Ricci *A Census of Caxtons* (Oxford 1909) pp. 85–6; T. F. Dibdin *Joseph Ames' Typographical Antiquities* (London 1810–19) I 261–3; W. A. Copinger *Supplement to Hain's Repertorium Bibliographicum* (London 1895) III 4; Kaltenbacher *op. cit.* 348–9.

Introduction

il passa oultre. Et quant il fut oultre passe, il torna son cheval, si regarda vers celle part ou il avoit laisse Vienne et puis commenca a crier a haulte voiz: 'O Vienne, fleur de toute beaulte, fontaine de toute courtoisie et de toute loyaulte, et que pourray je desormais devenir, quant j'ay perdu la presence de vostre tres doulz et plaisant regart, ne veoir ne pourray vostre tres gracieuse pourtrayture? Helas, commant pourray je ma douleureuse vie passer?' Et en ce disant il luy vint si grant doleur au cueur, qu'il ne scavoit s'il estoit mort ou vif, ne s'il estoit nuyt ou jour, ains se pauma sur son cheval, si qu'il cheyt du cheval a terre. Et le cheval, qui se sent alegie, s'en va le grant chemyn vers Aigues Mortes.

Contrast this passage with the following accounts of the same episode. The first is from B.N. Fr. 20044 and the second from Leeu:

Et pource que mieulx vos souvienge de moy veez vos cy ung dyamant Et vous prie que vous le gardies pour lamour de moy Et puis le va baisier et embrasser auec moult grant souspirs et pleurs elle le consoloit le mieulx quelle pouoit en priant nostre Sieur que en brief le peult veoir ainsy comme son cuer desire Et adont Paris sen partit de Vienne et tint son chemin toult seul auec son varlet souspirant et en grant douleur de son cuer Et vint jusques a la rivere quil nauoyent peu passer Et quasi demy despere ne douta rien & entra dedans leaue fust baisse Et luy et son varlet passerent sans nul mal car il nosoyent passer pas les villes et ainsy alla joucques en Aigues Mortes

Et affin que mieulx vous souuienge de moy/ vez cy ung anel dor ou il y a ung dyamant/ lequel ie vous prie que le vueillez garder pour lamour de moy. (End of chapter.)
Comment paris se partit de Vienne/ et le laissa en leglise Apres beaucoup daultres langaiges il baisa Vienne en moult grans souspirs & plaintes/ et elle se confortoit le mieulx quelle pouoit/ en priant nostre seigneur ihesucrist que en brief temps le peust veoir comme son cueur le desiroit plus que riens que au monde fust Et alors paris se departit de Vienne auec grant dueil et tristesse Si print son chemin luy et son varlet tant quilz vindrent iusques a la riuiere ou ilz nauoient peut passer/ et comme desespere quil estoit ne doubta riens/ mais entra dedens/ & leaue fut basse/ si que ilz passerent sans peril quelconque/ & cheuaucherent deux iours sans

menger/ car ilz nosoient passer par les villes Et ainsi il alla iusques en aigues mortes . . .

The passage in Caxton is as follows:

And to thende that ye the better remembre me loo here is a rynge of gold wyth a dyamonde/ the which I praye you that ye wyl kepe for the loue of me

¶ How Parys departed from Vyenne/ and lefte hyr in the chyrche/ After moche other langage paris kyssed vyenne wyth grete syghes and thoughtes/ and she comforted hym the best wyse she myght/ in prayeng our lord Ihesu Cryste that in short tyme she myght see hym/ lyke as hyr herte desyred moost of ony thynge that was in the world/ And thenne Parys departed fro Vyenne wyth grete sorowe and heuynesse/ And took his waye wyth hys seruaunte tyl he came to the ryuer where they coude not tofore haue passed/ and as despayred doubted noo thynge but entred therin/ and the water was soo aualed that they passed wythoute ony peryl/ And they rode two dayes wythoute ony mete/ for they durst not passe thurgh ony toun/ And they passed tyl they came to aygues mortes. (39/28 ff.)

The general differences between the two versions of the story are clearly illustrated by these passages. In addition to these general differences, important specific differences separate Version I from Version II. All texts of Version I are preceded by a rather long prologue, giving the general synopsis of the story, the statement that it was translated by Pierre de la Cypede, and the date, usually September 2, 1432. No text of Version II carries this prologue. It is so important for the history of the story and the dating and is so intrinsically interesting that I shall quote it in full as it is found in B.N. Fr. 1480.

Alain, qui moult fut saige, a escript au livre de ses doctrines une auctorite que dit en latin: hoc crede quod tibi verum esse videtur. Et veult autant dire ceste auctorite, extraicte du latin en francois — tu croyras les chouses que te resembleront estre veritables. Et pourtant je prantz cest teme en ceste part, pour ce que j'ai tout mon temps prins plaisir a lire romans et croniques des ystoyres enciennes, ainsi comme de la vie de Lanceloit et de Tristain, de

Introduction

Floriment, et de Guy de Berrant, qui moult firent de beaulx faitz en leur vie, selon que j'ay trouve escript. Et pluseurs chouses y ay trouvees qui moult sont impossibles a croyre. Pluseurs aultres livres ay je veu, mes entre les aultres j'ay tenu ung livre, escript en langaige prouvensal, qui fut extraist d'ung aultre livre, escript en langaige cathalain. Auquel livre se contenoit la vie d'ung baron, qui s'appelloit messire Godeffroy de Lanson, qui estoit dauphin de Vienne. Et eust une filhe, que l'om appelloit Vienne, laquelle estoit non pareilhe de beaulte. Et comme ung chivalier, qui s'appelloit Paris, filz d'ung baron que l'om nommoit messire Jaques, fust amoureux de ladicte Vienne, si que pour l'amour d'elle il fist en sa vie mains beaulx faitz, comme vous pourres ouyr sa avant. Et pourtant quar la matiere me semble estre bien raisonnable et asses creable, et aussi que l'ystoyre est asses plaisant, quar belle chouse est oyr raconpter les beaulx faitz que les enciens firent jadis, cy ay entrepris a vous estrayre l'ystoire du langaige provencal en francoys. Si veul requerir et supplier a tous ceulx qui cestuy livre liront, que ce ilz y trouvoyent escript aucune chouse que ne fust bien seant, que ilz veullent a mes defaulx pardonner et les reparer selon leur bon avisemant, quar mon sans n'est pas souffisant a telle besoigne bien traictier, et aussi que je ne suis pas Francoys de nature, ains fuz nes et nouris en la cite de Marcelle. Et c'il vous plaist savoir qui je suis: de Saint Piere j'ay prins le non, de la Cypede pour sournon. Et fut encommance a escripre cest livre l'an de grace mil CCCC trente deux le tiers jour du moys de septembre.

All texts of Version I begin with this prologue essentially as quoted. One (Carpentras) mentions a 'translator' other than Cypede, and one (B.N. Fr. 1479) mentions a scribe, guillem le moign. All give Pierre de la Cypede as the translator from Provençal into French.

A second specific difference between Version I and Version II is in the names of some of the characters. Version I calls the Bishop, the Bishop of St. Vincent; Version II calls him the Bishop of St. Laurent (i.e. Laurence). Version I calls Paris's aide Oliver; Version II calls him George. Finally, two less important differences should be noted. Version II mentions in the beginning that the events of the story took place in 1271. Version I makes no mention of a specific year, but both versions state that it was in the time of King Charles of

France. Scattered through Version I are five rather elaborately described dreams, all allegorical and all foreshadowing events to come; these are not found in Version II, although several texts contain vestigial remnants of them.

Version I is undoubtedly the older and Version II is a redaction of it. No manuscript of Version II is as old as those of Version I. (Of course it is possible that there were some, now lost, but the presumption is against it.) Version II is largely represented by printed texts; there are no early printed texts of Version I. Completely convincing evidence of the priority of Version I comes from a comparison of the two. Many details in Version II need the expanded account of Version I to explain them; motivation for parts of the action lacking in Version II is to be found in Version I.

The Origin and Date of the Story

In trying to determine the origin and date of the story we are confronted with several related problems. Was the story, as the prologue claims, translated from Provençal into French? If so, when? Was the original story in Catalan? Is there any internal evidence that would help in determining the origin and date of the original?

The prologue of de la Cypede which is found at the beginning of all Version I manuscripts expressly states that the story was drawn out of Provençal and into French by Pierre de la Cypede, a citizen of Marseilles. No Provençal version exists, but we have evidence to show that de la Cypede was telling the truth. Both Kaltenbacher and Coville notice that the Carpentras fragments (the oldest manuscripts of *Paris et Vienne*) contain verbal evidence of a Provençal original and that in later manuscripts these Provençal forms gradually disappear.[1] External evidence also exists that tends to establish de la Cypede's identity and to corroborate his statement that he was of Marseilles. In the fifteenth century a family by the name of de la Cypede was well known in Marseilles. One of this family was a Pierre de la Cypede who was made a Squire of the Stables by Louis II

[1] A. A. Coville *La vie intellectuelle dans les domaines d'Anjou-Provence de 1380–1435* (Paris 1941) pp. 481–91; Kaltenbacher *op. cit.* 362.

during his visit to Marseilles in 1385. Coville remarks: 'C'était sans doute un jeune homme, et rien ne s'oppose à voir en lui l'auteur de *Paris et Vienne*.' This Pierre de la Cypede may indeed be the person associated with our story. The date could be right; the place is right since he belongs to Provence. To be sure, no evidence has been discovered linking this Pierre de la Cypede with literature; yet the fact that the name is a rather rare one, that the translator says he was of Marseilles, that there was a Pierre de la Cypede at Marseilles at the time—all strongly suggest that the translator was indeed the Squire of Marseilles.[1]

Added evidence comes from the fact that two of the early manuscripts of *Paris et Vienne* are connected with, or make reference to, the Castle of Orgon in Provence. One (Arsenal 3000) was written there. The Carpentras fragments were from the library of Nicholas de Peiresc (1580–1637); de Peiresc was a native of Provence. He made extensive collections of Provençal antiquities of all sorts, including manuscripts. In short, the whole tradition and history of *Paris et Vienne* centres in Provence.

The French manuscripts are all very explicit about dates. Three name 1443 as the date the story was worked out of Provençal into French; three give the date as 1432. Among these latter is the Carpentras manuscript, which after indicating 1432 as the date de la Cypede translated the story into French, goes on to say that that manuscript was 'traylatie' by 'Inart beyssan' on the seventeenth of February, 1438. If Carpentras is of 1438—and I see no reason to doubt it—then 1443 is obviously too late for the translation into French. I believe that 1432 can be accepted on the basis of this evidence and the further fact that it would better fit the chronology of the life of Pierre de la Cypede, made Squire in 1385.

The statement of de la Cypede in the prologue that the Provençal text was drawn out of the Catalan tongue has been generally accepted by scholars in the past.[2] There seemed to be no more reason to doubt his word about this than about the

[1] See especially Coville *op. cit.* p. 485.
[2] Kaltenbacher expressed doubts *op. cit.* 363.

dates. But this is somewhat different. Here de la Cypede says simply (Carpentras prologue) '... jay tenu ung livre escript en langue provensal qui fut strait dun aultre libre escript en langue catelane...' There is no indication of the source of his information; it would seem not to be first-hand like that concerning the dates.

In spite of de la Cypede's statement that the original was in the Catalan language, the evidence—indirect to be sure—favours rather a Provençal or even French origin. The oldest manuscript is in French with a sprinkling of Provençal forms. No manuscripts of the story exist in Spanish or in Catalan, and there is no record of the existence of any early versions of the story in those languages. The printed texts in these languages are all late and all belong to Version II of the story. Against this we have the fact that Francisco Imperial referred to the story of *Paris and Vienne* in two poems in Spanish in 1405 and 1411, evidently expecting his Spanish readers to understand the reference.[1]

Important evidence of French or Provençal origin comes from the story itself. The action is localized in Vienne, a city in the south of France. Not only are the place-names all French, but so also are most of the personal names. This is true of all tellings of the story in all languages, including Catalan and Spanish. Early in the story occurs a long list of knights, defenders of the three fairest ladies of Europe: Florye, the daughter of the Duke of Normandy, Constance, the sister of the King of England, and Vienne, daughter of the Dauphin of Vienne. All these names are evidently inventions of the author, for none of them can be identified with any historical character; even some of the titles were devised by the author. All except Edward are French. The names in the list vary somewhat between Version I and Version II, but the list in Version II, though shorter, is likewise French. The lists in the Spanish and Catalan texts are almost identical with those in

[1] Francisque Michel *El cancionero de Juan Alfonso de Baena* (Leipzig 1860) I 199 and 239. Kaltenbacher felt that the dating of the story by reference to the reign of King Charles of France (all versions) was a sure indication of French or Provençal origin, since by the fourteenth century Spanish and Catalonian writers no longer recorded time according to the reigns of French kings. But of course the reference could have been added by the French translator.

Version II. No Spanish names appear. If the author were Spanish or Catalan he certainly would have included a few Spanish grandees as defenders of the beauty of Europe, even if he were telling a story of France. It is equally hard to believe that he would not have made one of the three most beautiful ladies of Europe a Spanish lady.

Moreover, the story is a very particular and realistic picture of the city of Vienne and its surroundings. We are told that the Dauphin lived adjacent to the church of Notre Dame. In the fifteenth century there was a church of Notre Dame adjacent to the Dauphin's palace.[1] The realistic description of the details of the palace and of the countryside, the account of Paris's drawing money from Messire Bertrand's bank, of the boatman and his craft, of the road and post stations to Aigues-Mortes traceable still today—all these details and many more of the same sort suggest an intimate personal knowledge on the part of the author of the city of Vienne, its local customs, and its environs.

To believe in a Spanish origin we would have to assume a Spanish version of *Paris and Vienne* probably very different from the one we now have; that the story was drastically altered as it passed from Spain to Provençal to make it completely French in detail, style and psychology; that as time went on all vestiges of the old story disappeared entirely in Spain; and finally that in the fifteenth century the Spanish borrowed the story back in its French form. All this seems highly improbable. Why then the reference by de la Cypede to a Catalan original? Such ascriptions were common enough in the Middle Ages to suggest antiquity, authority, exotic background. But that does not seem to be the purpose here. De la Cypede does not make a point of it; the reference is rather casual. Certainly one does not get the impression that de la Cypede is speaking from first-hand information. It might well be a mistake in the copy he

[1] See Léon Maître 'Vienne la sainte et ses premières églises' *Revue de l'art chrétien* XLIX (1906); Nicholas Chorier *Les recherches sur les antiquités de la ville de Vienne* (Vienne 1846) p. 53; C. Faure 'Histoire de la réunion de Vienne à la France (1328–1454)' *Bulletin de l'Académie Delphinale* Ser. IV, xix (1905) 327–501; Ser. IV, xx 13.

was translating. In spite of this reference I still feel sure that the original was French and that the Spanish and other texts of the story are derivative.

As one reads the story and notes the numerous specific references to historical characters and to events, such as the Crusades, it strikes one that the story might be localized and dated from internal evidence. We are told that it took place in the reign of King Charles of France, that the Dauphin of Vienne, a main character in the story, was Geoffrey de Lanson, that the king had a son Louis. In the list of noblemen attending the tournament are some twenty-five names, including Edward, son of the King of England. Constance, sister of the King of England, is one of the three ladies whose beauty inspires the knights of England. Pope Innocent proclaims a crusade and Geoffrey de Lanson is sent to spy out the land in preparation for it.

It is impossible, however, to identify these characters with historical persons. Several kings of France in the Middle Ages were named Charles, but only one had a son Louis, and he was Charles the Simple, who died in 898. Several sons of English kings bore the name of Edward, but none of them had an aunt named Constance. No Geoffrey de Lanson can be identified as either Dauphin of Vienne or member of the Crusade of Pope Innocent III (d. 1216), the only Pope Innocent associated with a crusade. The names of the knights who take part in the tournament seem to be imaginary, since none can be identified. Some bear imaginary titles. This evidence would tend to prove that the story as a whole is pure invention and one in which the author has been to some pains to make sound as authentic as possible, for by the end of the Middle Ages the audience of romances was beginning to look for stories in which the matter was 'reasonable and tolerably credible'.

Anyone familiar with medieval story will recognize at once in *Paris and Vienne* a number of stock situations: the knight fighting incognito in the tournament, the religious as intermediary between the lovers, the elopement, the ring token, the exile and return theme, the rescue of the prisoner by getting the jailer drunk, the disguise of the hero, the ruse by which the heroine avoids an unwanted marriage. To be sure, other incidents of a more specific and a more realistic nature are to be found, such as the serenade, Vienne's mother's visit to the castle of Messire Jacques, the thwarting of the elopement by the impassable river and the punishment of Vienne which follows. But these are rather incidental; it is the stock motifs that carry the story. A skilled artificer, like the one behind *Cliges* or *Ipomedon*, combined the old with the new to produce a story of high plausibility; everything in the story suggests a man who had detailed knowledge of Provence and southern France, and drew freely on that knowledge.

One piece of objective evidence carries the date of the story definitely into the fourteenth century. Kaltenbacher first pointed out that reference is made to *Paris and Vienne* in two poems of the Spanish poet Francisco Imperial, *En dos sete çientos é mas doss é tres* (1405) and *Muchos poetas leý* (1411).[1] In the first of these poems Paris and Vienne are included in a list which mentions many famous heroes and heroines of romance: Tristan, Lancarote, Amadis, Oryana, Blancaflor, Flores. These references suggest that Paris and Vienne were well known to Francisco Imperial's audience as early as 1405, and that they were almost proverbial as lovers; in short, that the story was in Spanish in Spain as early as 1400. But that assumes that an author always uses the well known for an illustration, that he never introduces the unfamiliar. Francisco Imperial was of Italian blood; he was born in Genoa, the son of a Genoese jeweller. The family moved to Seville, where Francisco spent his youth. Later he spent much time in the land of his birth and became widely educated in Italian culture. A student of Dante, he introduced that poet to Spain. He not only read Italian and Spanish, but also French and Arabic and probably English. One can consequently argue that Francisco Imperial knew Paris and Vienne from French, Provençal, or Italian sources, as he probably knew Lancelot, Floris, etc., rather than from Spanish. Francisco Imperial brought general European culture into Spain. The reference to Paris and Vienne, then,

[1] See pp. 362–3. For a general account of Francisco Imperial see J. Fitzmaurice Kelly *History of Spanish Literature* (London 1921) pp. 97–8.

tells us nothing about the existence of the story in Spanish at an early period; it does, of course, prove that *Paris and Vienne* was composed before 1400.

Caxton and the Story in French

Caxton's *Paris and Vienne* is very close to the version printed by Leeu and to that in B.N. Fr. 20044; in fact many passages are verbally identical in all three texts. The following are typical of hundreds of such passages:

And whan vyenne herde alle the mynstrellys of the londe
Et quant Vienne ouyt ces menestries

that sowned at þ^t feste she sayd to ysabel hyr damoysel & preuy felowe
qui sonnoit ensemble a celle feste va dire a ysabel, sa compaigne

by my fayth swete syster these mynstrellys playen nouȝt
Par my foy, ma doulce seur, ses menestries ne sonent

to the regarde of them that were wonte to come before our chambre . . . (4/6–10)
sauf a comparason que viennent en notre chambre . . .

And Parys gaf to geffroy so grete a stroke that hys hors
Mais Paris donna si grant coup a Geoffray que le cheval a Geoffray

slode and thenne Geffroy ouerthrewe to the erthe but by cause
eslata dessous. Et Geoffray tumba a terre mais pour que

that the hors slode it was sayd that the hors was cause that he ouerthrewe . . . (16/4–7)
le cheval eslata fut dit que faute du cheval estoit tumba . . .

When the Erle of flaunders had redde the letters of
Qant le conts de Flaundres eust recu le lettre du

the doulphyn & vnderstood that he wold marye his doughter vyenne
daulphin et entendoit quil voulloit marier sa fille Vienne

whych was of the age of xv yere he trayted that she shold haue
quelle estoit le age de xv ans. Et traita quelle eust

of two barons that one that is to wete the sone of the kyng of
des deus barons l'ung ou le filz du roy

englond or the sone of the duke of bourgoyne . . . (44/10–15)
d'angleterre ou le filz du duc de bourgogne . . .

Introduction xxiii

Dozens of passages such as these are to be found in every chapter; they suggest that Caxton used a transcription of the story very close to the source of Leeu and B.N. Fr. 20044. This is further established by the carry-over of many French words from these texts directly into English. Frequently Caxton carries over the French word by linking it with a common English synonym: derke and obscure 54/3=Fr. *obscure et tenebreuse*; trystesse and sorowe 10/9=Fr. *tristesse*; menace and thretene 42/21=Fr. *menace*; Ioyaulx or Iewels 13/27=Fr. *joyaulx*; chyef & hede 19/1=Fr. *chief*; feures or accesse 21/10=Fr. *accesse*; vayssal and subget 23/30=Fr. *vaissal*; vysage ne chere 48/2=Fr. *chere*; achyeued and fynysshed 56/29=Fr. *achyue*; sory & dolant 19/13=Fr. *dolant*. This list could easily be extended. The point here is to show that Caxton was working with a text so close to Leeu's edition and that of B.N. Fr. 20044 that it alone could furnish him with these words in their respective contexts.

Caxton also carried over literally many French idioms from this text: quasi half in despayr 25/23=Fr. *quasi de demy despare*; took terme 30/4=Fr. *prisent terme*; felonnye (anger)= Fr. *felonnie*; quasi al abasshed 31/12=Fr. *quasi toult esbahy*; knyghtes hardy and valyaunte (adj. after noun) 11/1 =Fr. *chevaliers hardi & valliant*. Many French words are lifted over bodily without translation or linking: e.g. egal, subget, loenge (Fr. *louange*), indigne, truffes, veray god (Fr. *vrai dieu*).

Several mistranslations result in lack of meaning. Paris asks his father to ask the Dauphin for Vienne as his wife. Messire Jacques is distressed: 'Et luy dist en le reprouvant quil ne parlast plus de cela car il ne voulloit mourir pour sa folie et quil luy demandast aultre chose.' Caxton follows the French closely, even to preserving the French idiom *en reprouvant*, but he misreads *folie*, taking it to be *fille*, and so translates 'he sayd in repreuyng hym that he neuer shold speke more of that fayte for he wold not deye for hys *doughter*' (31/37ff.). In another context Caxton omitted a word, with the result that the English sentence makes little sense. George, preparing for the flight of Paris and Vienne, 'loua une gallee et establit en toulx les passaiges cheuaux . . .' The French is clear enough, but Caxton missing *cheuaux* translates 'he hyred a galeye and establisshed al the passages' (35/16f.).

It is not necessary to multiply instances showing Caxton's close connection with this French text; that is obvious in every sentence. But though there is this constant identity of sentence, idiom, and word, one discovers on detailed examination that there are certain differences in Caxton, Leeu, and B.N. Fr. 20044 which make one conclude that all derive from a common text and that B.N. Fr. 20044 is closer to that text than Caxton and Leeu are. In general Caxton varies, as the notes will indicate, with Leeu against the MS. It must be stressed, however, that these differences are usually verbal, and that the three accounts are practically the same. If we did not have Leeu we would conclude that Caxton was translating from the French MS. or its intermediate source.

One can never be sure, of course, that a variation in Caxton is not deliberate on Caxton's part. Caxton's chapter headings, for example, are often different from those in the French MS. and from those in Leeu, and they sometimes occur at different places. Remembering Caxton's habit of re-ordering his material and his fondness for writing headings, one is inclined to think that these differences are deliberate on Caxton's part. Likewise, here and there in the Caxton are expressions like 'now sayth thystory'. These are usually lacking in both the French texts, but they are natural enough additions in the English translation. The missing and the damaged portions of B.N. Fr. 20044 do not help us much. To be sure, those portions of the story are in Caxton and in Leeu, but this does not necessarily prove that Caxton was using another text or that he was using Leeu, since the mutilation is such that it might have occurred later.

Two significant passages of considerable length are found in B.N. Fr. 20044 and not in Caxton and Leeu. The longest, 40 lines in the French MS., occurs at 70/36 of the present text. This tells of the distress of Paris (still disguised as a Moor) at the Dauphin's not recalling his oath to give him whatever he demanded when they should be safe home in Vienne. Paris summons the *frère* and tells him to go to the Dauphin, remind

Introduction

him of his promise and demand his daughter as wife for Paris. When the *frère* bears this message to the Dauphin, he readily agrees, but expresses doubt that Vienne will consent and he suggests that the *frère* and the Bishop of St. Laurence speak to Vienne. This is all omitted in Caxton and in Leeu. Instead

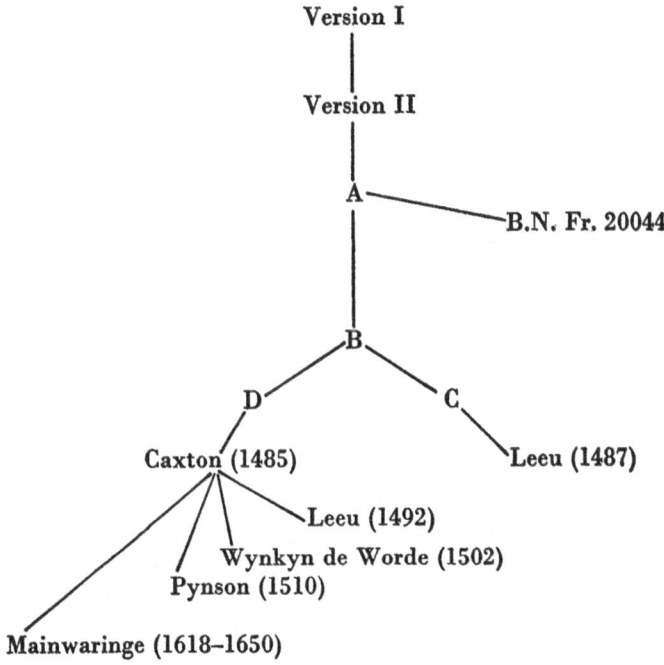

the Dauphin asks Paris (disguised as a Moor) if he would have Vienne as his wife; Paris answers yes. In other words, in the English and in Leeu the Dauphin initiates the matter and the whole is condensed into one line. (Version I contains the episode as it is in B.N. Fr. 20044, but much expanded.) Since Leeu and the other members of Version II agree with Caxton against B.N. Fr. 20044, it would appear that this condensation is not the work of Caxton and that Caxton is, therefore, using a closely allied text rather than B.N. Fr. 20044. This is confirmed by a similar omission at 76/10.

xxvi *Introduction*

Nor can Caxton be translating the source of Leeu. Though Caxton's text again and again agrees with Leeu against B.N. Fr. 20044 even to the smallest verbal unit, there are a number of readings in which they are different. Frequently, especially in the beginning, Leeu and B.N. Fr. 20044 agree against Caxton. These differences are fundamental and not just changes traceable to the translator (e.g. 2/11, 2/15, 2/32, 6/5—all variations are listed in the Notes).

These relations may be diagrammatically indicated by the figure on page xxv.[1]

Caxton as a Translator

An examination of Caxton's translations beginning with his first, *Recuyell of the Historyes of Troy*, 1474, reveals that Caxton constantly grew in accuracy, mastery of idiom, and ease of style. The *Recuyell* is full of trivial errors of translation; and its English has faults in abundance—faults which Caxton never entirely overcame, but which diminish through the years: redundancy, tendency to carry over the idiom of the original, lack of feeling for English syntax. But Caxton grew so much in skill as a translator and in competence as a prose stylist between 1474 and 1489 when he translated *Blanchardyn and Eglantine* that the modern editor of this work praises him as 'not inferior to Peacock, the greatest prosaist of his time'.[2] The translation of *Paris and Vienne* was finished on August 31, 1485; it belongs, therefore, to the period of Caxton's maturity.

Except for two or three passages the translation is completely accurate and although Caxton still shows a tendency to make a kind of French-English by lifting words from French into English and by translating French idioms literally, *Paris and Vienne* compares very favourably with the best narrative prose of the century. Its faults are the faults of the prose of the period: redundancy, especially in the use of two close synonyms (often one French and one English); tangled

[1] For a detailed account of the relations of all the various texts of the story to one another see Kaltenbacher *op. cit.* 361.
[2] Leon Kellner, ed. *Blanchardyn and Eglantine* EETS ES LVIII p. cxi.

sentence structure; uncertain word order; mixture of indirect and direct discourse.

This practice of using two or more synonyms is probably the most common characteristic of fifteenth-century prose style, both French and English. It is one of the methods by which style was 'enriched' or 'adorned'. Lydgate did much to set the pattern for the century in English; he was not only motivated by the idea of enriching his style but also by the idea of enlarging the vocabulary by introducing new words from French and Latin. This practice became so common that it finally came to be a literary convention. Caxton used it freely. Like Lydgate he felt that such doublets added immeasurably to the literary qualities of a piece of writing, and like Lydgate too he was concerned with introducing new words into English. Then, too, one must not forget that Caxton's original often followed such a stylistic pattern and that Caxton usually carried over what he found.

Paris and Vienne does not contain as many examples of this construction as do the earlier works. There are, however, enough to impress even a casual reader. They fall into three categories: (*a*) doublets or triplets, literally translated; (*b*) one element from French retained and joined to an English synonym; (*c*) deliberate devising of doublets by Caxton when there are none in the original. An analysis of the frequency of occurrence of these types shows that (*b*) outnumbers the others two to one; the percentage of (*b*) is forty-nine. The first type —direct transfer of both elements from French—occurs in twenty per cent of the cases. There are very few instances of doublets in French translated by a single word or phrase in English. One observes from these expressions that there exists a tendency towards conventional association of pairs like the clichés in ballad or romance style; consequently a number of these appear more than once.

I have given above in another connection[1] some examples of these expressions. A few more here will illustrate the various types: (*a*) wayle and syghe 10/3 · Fr. *plaindre et souspirer*; trystesse and sorowe 10/9 · Fr. *paine et doleur*; trouble and

---

[1] p. xxiii.

dyscorde 11/11 · Fr. *mal et dommage*; wepe & waylle 19/20 · Fr. *plourer et souspirer*; hauyng grete Indygnacyon and alle angry 33/4 · Fr. *tant indigne et couroucie*; pensyf and ymagynatyf 40/13 · Fr. *en pencement et ymaginacion*; prowesse and hardynes 2/27 · Fr. *proesse et hardiesse*. (b) wytte and entendement 12/8 · Fr. *entendement*; bruyt & renomme 9/24 · Fr. *bruyt*; shone and resplendysshed 13/28 · Fr. *resplendissient*; armed & apparaylled 13/37 · Fr. *appareille*; sygne & token 18/13 · Fr. *signe*; sory & dolant 19/13 · Fr. *dolant*; amytye and loue 19/36 · Fr. *amour*; feures or accesse 21/10 · Fr. *accesse*; where [he] was and laye 21/21 · Fr. *estoit*; orysons and prayers 25/20 · Fr. *orison*; grewe and encreaced 2/4 · Fr. *croissoit*; to wyf and in maryage 31/34 · Fr. *pour fame*; wrath & rancour 35/3 · Fr. *maleulence*; reioyced & Ioyous 67/7 · Fr. *print plaisir*; menace and thretene 42/21 · Fr. *menace*; pure and clene of hyr body 41/11 · Fr. *pure de son corps*; tryste & pensyful 6/2 · Fr. *triste*. (c) doublets original with Caxton: wele & prouffyt 51/8; appyereth & sheweth 1/14; gladnes & Ioye 1/23; honour & Ioye 1/24 · Fr. *en molt grant noblesse*; a nonne or a menchon 33/12; mayntened hym ne susteyned 16/11; sawe and byhelde 27/23; reputed and holden 11/23; brake & shewed 3/12 · Fr. *au quil il disoit tout couraige*; to wete & knowe 3/31.

There is only one attempt to 'embellish' the style in any other way than by studding it with French words. That is at line 3/2 where, after saying that Paris 'knewe nought of amorouste', he adds 'but not longe after Venus the goddes of loue fyred his thouȝt with the hert vnto a noble yong lady'.

As we turn from a consideration of diction to that of syntax, we find that Caxton shows the same general tendency to follow his original rather literally. The first problem that confronts one in trying to untangle Caxton's syntax is punctuation. Caxton here uses only one mark of punctuation, the /. This functions as a comma, as a semicolon, and as a full-stop. In addition, it is often used to mark a break in the thought, to set off direct discourse from indirect, and now and then sheer accident or whimsicality dictates its use. For this reason it is often very difficult to tell where Caxton would stop a sentence, what elements are restrictive, and what co-ordinate. Capitalization does not help in fixing the sentence, for that too follows no regular pattern.

When one takes Caxton's running lines here in *Paris and Vienne* and punctuates them according to sense, one discovers that much of what seems to be faulty sentence structure is cleared up. This is not true of Caxton's earlier translations, for in them the syntax is often hopelessly confused. Editors of Caxton have found that Caxton's greatest sentence weakness is excessive subordination, the tendency to link subordinate clause to subordinate clause until the reader is led farther and farther away from the central idea. Sentences like the following from *Paris and Vienne* 49/22 are very common in Caxton's earlier work, '. . . to put in pryson hyr that is soo noble a creature/ whyche is ful of al vertues/ that is the fayre vyenne/ whyche is noo thynge cause of thys fayte . . .' There is some but not much of this in *Paris and Vienne*. Caxton's later works show that he had become aware of the principle of subordination, and consequently he generally makes subordinate ideas subordinate in form.

In *Paris and Vienne* Caxton shows more awareness of the difference between direct and indirect discourse than he did in his earlier works. In the early works he passes without indication from one to the other, but of course such confusion is common in the prose of the period in both English and French. By the end of the fifteenth century, writers were beginning to be more careful to differentiate between direct and indirect discourse by sentence form and syntax. Only nine instances of such confusion are to be found in *Paris and Vienne* and five of them are direct translations from the French. In several instances Caxton keeps his form consistent in English though his French original does not. The following example is typical: '. . . he kyssed hyr & sette on her hede the crowne whyche the kynge had gyuen hym/ and tolde to hyr how she had goton the honour for to be the moost fayrest damoysell of the world/ and loo here is the fayr crowne that the quene of fraunce sendeth to you . . .' (18/18–22).

These then are the general characteristics of Caxton's prose, characteristics that belong as much to the period as to Caxton individually. But in spite of them, one is impressed in *Paris and Vienne* by the clear, straightforward style. I would not agree that Caxton is 'as great a prosaist as Peacock', for he lacks Peacock's logical articulation of thoughts, his rich vocabulary, and his polish. And he is not as great a prosaist as Malory, for he lacks Malory's balance, concreteness, and ease. Caxton's greatest faults as a stylist and as a translator come from his naïve belief that he must construe his original as literally as possible. Again and again the French is represented word for word in Caxton's English and in the original French order. To us today this often adds a touch of quaintness pleasing in a fifteenth-century romance, but no doubt it would have struck Peacock as timid and slavish.

Caxton is more inclined to freer expression and more inclined to take liberties with his original in passages expressing the author's opinion, and in descriptive and in expository passages. Dialogue he translates literally. His knowledge of French is accurate and sure; rarely does he make a mistake and, when he does, one is inclined to think that hasty reading (like the omission of a *ne*) or difficult handwriting was the cause.

Caxton makes some deliberate changes and additions. In French Paris's father refers to the Bishop of St. Laurence as *le dyable devesque*, because the Bishop, he thinks, is seducing Paris away from a knightly life into a religious one. Caxton, evidently feeling that the word *dyable* is a bit too strong, drops it. He is inclined to add an adjective like 'blessed' or 'gloryous' to the French Christ or Virgin. When the French mentions God alone, Caxton is likely to add 'to the glorious vyrgyn marye' (as 18/35). He adds a sentence to 62/28 telling that the Pope and the King of France tried to ransom the Dauphin; in French they leave him to his fate. He makes the Dauphin say (33/11f.) that he would rather his daughter became a nun than married Paris; in French the Dauphin says he would rather she was dead. Here and there Caxton adds a phrase in glorification of chivalry, or of England, or of the aristocracy. French counts become earls in Caxton; barons become princes. He tells of Paris being dubbed knight (2/18); there is no mention of such a ceremony in French. Caxton shows his acquaintance with the etiquette of the tournament by mentioning the establishing of the *lystes* (6/5).

Note

In the text instances of the abbreviation stroke for *n* are expanded without notice.

All misprints except *u* for *n* and *n* for *u* are corrected and the original form given in a note. Misprints involving *n* and *u* are corrected without notice. They are as follows: (*n* for *u*) *hane* 4/37; *tonrnoyment* 10/22; *pnyssaunte* 18/27; *hnmbly* 27/19; *sernyce* 28/10; *demannde* 29/13; *dnellyd* 49/36; *hanyng* 56/2; *commannded* 62/21; *hane* 62/29; *fanlconner* 64/28; *syngnler* 71/34. (*u* for *n*) *Mouutferat* 6/28; *coustaunce* 11/6; *breuues* 15/15; *breunes* 15/18, 15/19; *carues* 15/25; *ayeust* 33/20; *couuceyl* 38/5; *uo* 52/3; *faulconuers* 60/1.

Chapter headings are here set in italic type to distinguish them from the text proper. Caxton uses the same type for both.

Signature numbers follow folios to which they refer.

[PARIS AND VIENNE]

¶ *Here begynneth thystorye of the noble ryght valyaunt & worthy knyght Parys/ and of the fayr Vyenne the daulphyns doughter of vyennoys/ the whyche suffred many aduersytees bycause of theyr true loue or they coude enioye the effect therof of eche other/*

In the tyme of kynge Charles of Fraunce the yere of our lord Ihesu Cryst M CC lxxj/ was in the londe of vyennoys a ryche baron daulphyn and lord of the lond that was named syr Godefroy of alaunson & was of the kynges kynrede of fraunce/ the whiche daulphyn was ryȝt myghty and a grete 5 lord bothe in hauoyr and in landes/ & was a ryght wyse man/ in so moche that for his grete wysedom he was moche made of/ bothe of the kynge of fraunce & of al the lordes & barons of his courte/ soo that noo thynge was doon in the sayd royame but that he was called therto/ & had to his wyf 10 a moche fayre lady whiche cleped was dame dyane whyche was of so grete beaulte that she was wel worthy & dygne to be named after that fayre sterre þᵗ men calle dyane that appyereth & sheweth a lytel afore the day/ and also she was replenysshed of all noblenes & gentylnes that a lady may or 15 ought to haue/ The sayd daulphyn thenne and this noble lady dyane were vij yere to gyder wythoute yssue that moche they desyred to haue/ and prayed our lord bothe nyght & day that they myght haue chyldren playsaunt and redy to hys deuyne seruyce/ and our lord thorugh hys benygnyte herde 20 theyr prayer/ and after hys playsyr gaf vnto them the viij yere of theyr maryage a ryght fayr doughter for the whyche/ grete gladnes & Ioye was made thorugh all the daulphyns londe/ and the chylde was baptysed with grete honour & Ioye/ & in token of grete loue they named hyr vyenne by cause 25 the cyte where she was borne in was called vyenne/ and thys doughter was delyuerd vnto a noble lady for to be nourysshed wyth hyr/ the whyche lady was of the sayd cyte and had a lytel doughter of the age of vyenne the whyche was named

[*Paris and Vienne*]

ysabel/ & so the fayre vyenne was nourysshed wyth the same ysabel from hyr tender age vnto many yere after/ & soo grete loue was bytwene them bothe that they called eche other systers/ & the fayre vyenne grewe and encreaced euer in souerayn beawte & gentylnesse/ so that the renomee of hyr excellent beawte flourysshed not onely thurgh al fraunce but also thurgh al the Royame [a j^r] of englond & other contrees/ It happed after she was xv yere of age that she was desyred to maryage of many kny3tes & grete lordes/ & at that tyme was in the daulphyns courte emonge many hys kny3tes/ a noble man of auncyent lygnage & of fayr londes/ the whiche was wel byloued of the daulphyn & of alle the lordes of the lande and was called syr Iames/ thys noble man had a moche fayr sone that had to name Parys/ & hys fader made hym to be taught in al good custommes/ and whan he was xviij yere of age he was adressed to the dyscyplyne of armes/ & demened hym self so nobly & worthely in al maner dedes of chyualrye that wythin a shorte tyme after he was doubed knyght by the hande of the sayd lord daulphyn/ ¶ Noo fayte of knyghthode ne none aduenture of chyualrye happed after but that he founde hym self at it in soo moche that the renommee of hym ranne thurgh al the world & men sayd he was one of the best kny3tes þ^t myght be founde in ony contree/ & helde hym self ryght clene in armes and lyued chastly & Ioyefully/ & had euer aboute hym fowles hawkes and houndes for hys dysporte to alle maner of huntyng suffysaunt ynough for a duc or for an erle/ and thurgh hys prowesse and hardynes he was acqueynted & knowen of many other grete lordes/ and emonge alle other he was gretely and louyngly acqueynted with a yonge knyght of the cyte of vyenne that hyght Edward/ and were bothe of one age and moche loued eche other/ and as two brethern of armes wente euer to gyder there as they knewe ony Ioustyng or appertyse of armes to be had for to gete honour/ ¶ And wete it wel that besyde theyr worthynes in armes they were good musycyens playeng vpon alle maner Instrumentes of musyke/ and coude synge veray wel/ but Parys passed in al poyntes[1] his felowe Edward/ Notwythstondyng Edward was

---

[1] ponytes C.

[Paris and Vienne] 3

amerous al redy of a noble lady of the courte of braban/ but
Parys as yet knewe nought of amorouste but not longe after
Venus the goddes of loue fyred his thouȝt with the hert vnto
a noble yong lady/ that is to wete the fayre vyenne the
daulphyns doughter of vyennoys that was his lyege lord/ & 5
the more he growed toward his flouryng age þe more he was
esprysed & brennyng of her loue for the grete beaute þt was
in hyr/ But Parys thought euer in hys herte that this loue
was not wel lykly ne cordable/ ¶ For he was not of so hyghe
lygnage as the noble mayden [a jv] vyenne was of/ & therfore 10
Parys kept hys loue secrete that none shold perceyue it sauf
Edward his trusty felowe to whom he brake & shewed his
counceyl And the fayre vyenne perceyued not that parys was
amerous of hyr/ nor parys also durst neyther shewe nor say
nothynge to hyr of hyt/ but the more that he sawe hyr the 15
more grewe þe fyre of loue within hym self/

¶ *How Parys and Edward hys felowe played wyth dyuers Instru-*
mentes by nyght tofore the chambre of vyenne/

Parys thenne & edward wythe one accorde dysposed them
self for to gyue somme melodyous myrthe to the noble
mayde vyenne/ and wyth theyr musycal Instrumentes/
as recourders/ they yede by nyght tyme to gyder toward that 20
parte of the castel where as the fayre vyenne laye in hyr
chambre/ and there they sange ful swetely and sowned
melodyously theyr musycal Instrumentes and pypes/ and
certeyn the melodye of their songes and the sowne of theyr
Instrument was so playsaunt & so swete that it passed al 25
other melodye/ And whan the daulphyn and his wyf & the
fayre vyenne theyr doughter herde this swete and melodyous
sowne/ as wel of mans wyces as of dyuers Instrumentes they
had grete Ioye and took grete playsyr at it & had grete desyre
to knowe what they were that so grete solace and Ioye made 30
tofore theyr castel/ and for to wete & knowe what they were
the daulphyn assygned a day of a feste at the whyche he sente
for alle maner mynstrellys in hys londe/ chargyng theym vpon

grete payne that they shold come for to playe before hym and
hys barons in his castel of vyenne/ & whan they were al come
they played and sange in theyr best wyse/ but emong them
were not founde tho mynstrelles that the lord daulphyn sought
fore/ wherof he was sorouful & desyred more to knowe what 5
they were than he dyd afore/ And whan vyenne herde alle
the mynstrellys of the londe that sowned at þᵗ feste she sayd
to ysabel hyr damoysel & preuy felowe/ by my fayth swete
syster these mynstrellys playen nouȝt to the regarde of them
that were wonte to come before our chambre/ & me dysplayseth 10
moche that I may not knowe them/ for certeynly they come
not hyther for nought/ for they loue outher you or me/

Whan the daulphyn vnderstode hys doughters wordes
he wyllyng to playse hyr sayd vnto hyr that yf it
were possyble she shold knowe what they were that 15
soo [a ijʳ] sange euery nyght before hyr chambre/ wherfore he
ordeyned x men of armes and commaunded them to hyde
them self pryuely there as the sowne was herde/ & that they
shold brynge to hym other by force or otherwyse them that
made that swete melodye/ Now came the nyght that the ij 20
yonge knyghtes Parys & Edward that no thynge knewe of
thembusshement that was layed for them came with theyr
Instrumentes toward the castel & there they began to synge
& sowned theyr Instrumentes so melodyously that grete
playsyr it was to here/ & whan they had songe and wold 25
haue retorned thyder as they were come fro/ the x knyghtes
lepte & cam forth and salewed them curtoyslle sayeng that
they nedes must come wyth them for to speke with their lord
the daulphyn/ Thenne sayd Parys to them/ Fayr lordes abyde
a lytel whyle/ yf it playse you & of vs ye shal haue an ansuer 30

Thenne wente Parys & edward a parte and spake to gyder/ ye
see fayr brother sayd Parys to Edward in what party we be
now and I wold not that ye shold haue by me ony dysplaysyr
nor harme/ but soo moche I telle you that or I shold suffre
me to be ledde tofore the daulphyn I had leuer deye/ therfore 35
fayr brother aduyse we what is beste for to do/ & edward
heryng parys wordes sayd/ brother myn haue noo fere of no

thynge and lete vs doo as ye wyl/ Thenne sayd they to the
x men of armes lordes thurgh your curtosye suffre vs to retorne
thyder as we came fro/ for we be at my lord the daulphyns
playsyr & of all the lordes & barons of his courte but in ony
maner as for thys tyme we may not fulfylle hys commaunde- 5
ment/

Whan the sayd x men of armes saw the ij knyghtes
dysobeyssaunt/ they ansuerd to them ye shal now
come to hym other wyth your wylle or by force/ and
bygan to pulle oute theyr swerdes & came ayenst the two 10
yonge knyghtes that naked were from al armes sauf theyr
swerdes and theyr bowclers/ wherwyth they couerd them
and so manfully deffended theyr bodyees that they hurte &
wounded sore al the ten armed men in so moche that they
maad them alle to voyde and flee fro the place whether they 15
wold or not/ ¶And on the morowe erly the ten men of armes
came tofore the daulphyn alle wounded and sore hurt/ And
they recounted to hym how two yonge men onely had arayed
them so and how they nedes must flee for fere of theyr lyues/
[a ij^v] 20
 wherof the daulphyn was ryght angry to see them so sore
hurt & took grete dysplaysyr of it/ and thought wel that
the sayd two yonge knyghtes were of grete strengthe and
vertue/ wherfore he comanded an hondred men to be redy
for to espye & take them the nyght folowyng yf they came 25
ageyn chargyng that none hurte shold be doon to them/ but
after theyr songe doon/ they shold be brought vnto hym/ but
thys enterpryse came to none effect/ for the two yonge
knyghtes came not ageyn but kepte alle that they had doon
secrete/ whan the fayre vyenne sawe that she my3t not knowe 30
what these mynstrellys were she thought they were somme
grete lordes that were amerous of hyr/ & she & hyr damoysel
ysabel spake of none other thynge than of these mynstrelles
and had grete playsyr to talke of them/ Parys seyng he durst
not say nor shewe the grete loue that he had to the fayr 35
vyenne/ thought he wold hyde hys courage from hyr/ wherfore
he took acqueyntaunce wyth the bysshop of Saynt Laurence

[*Paris and Vienne*]

the whyche lerned hym holy scrypture/ The daulphyn thenne seyng hys doughter ful tryste & pensyful for thys that she myght not knowe the sayd mynstrelles that so melodyously played tofore hyr chambre/ he ordeyned a Ioustyng place wythin his cyte of vyenne and made lystes and scaffoldes to 5 be sette vp & sente his herauldes in fraunce in Englond and in normandye to anounce & shewe vnto al kny3tes and gentylmen that wold doo faytes of armes and of chyualrye for loue of al ladyes and damoyselles/ that the Ioustes shold be holden the fyrst day of may/ in the cyte of vyenne/ And he that shold 10 doo best in armes/ shold haue of the Daulphyns doughter a shelde of crystalle of grete valure[1]/ and a garlond wyth roses and floures of fyn gold/ And wete ye wel that vyenne the noble and fayr mayden was ryght gladde of the Ioustes that hyr fader ordeyned for hyr sake/ Fro grete talent and desyre 15 she had to knowe hym that was soo amerous of hyr/ and she thought he wold be at the sayd fyrst day of may at vyenne/

¶ After the messagers that had pronounced the Ioustes were comen ageyn to the cyte of vyenne/ the moost parte of the knyghtes and gentylmen of the Royame of Fraunce of Englond 20 and of Normandye made them redy for to come to the cyte of Vyenne to the sayd Ioustes/ ¶ And in especyal many noble barons of the royame of Englond & of france that amerous [a iij^r] were of the fayre vyenne for the renomme of hyr grete beaulte/ came to the sayd Ioustes wyth ryche and noble araye/ 25 emonge whome was Iohan duc of bourbon neuew to the kyng of fraunce Edward the kynges sone of englond/ Anthony sone to the erle of prouence/ Gherard the marquys sone of Mountferat/ and wyllyam sone to the duc of Carnes/ Paris thenne knowyng this noble assemble and the Ioustes that shold be 30 the fyrst day of May thought in hym self whether he shold goo thyder or not/ but the grete loue that he had to the fayre vyenne constrayned hym therto/ Neuertheles he took counceyl of Edward his felowe the whyche answerd to hym/ yf ye goo I wyl holde you companye thyder/ but we must departe 35 secretly that we be not knowen/ and anone they made redy theyr harnoys & pourueyed theym of good horses whiche they harneysed al in whyt/ & none other token they had on them

[1] valurr C.

[Paris and Vienne]

whereby they myght be knowen sauf that they were arayed
al in whyt & one lyke that other/ The day of the Ioustes
thenne approched & al the lordes & barons afore sayd cam ij
dayes before the feste to þe cyte of vyenne where the daulphyn
for loue of them dyd doo make a noble scaffold where as the 5
fayre vyenne was rychely arayed/ & al that sawe hyr were
ameruaylled of hyr grete beaute To that feste came many
noble knyghtes & squyers clothed and arayed rychely after
the guyse of theyr contree/ & there were many mynstrellys
playeng vpon al maner Instrumentes/ & many good syngars 10
whyche the noble mayde vyenne herkened ful wel For hyr
hert was onely sette to thynke how she myght knowe hym
that was hyr louer/ parys thenne came thyder and was
ordeyned for to serue at the daulphyns table where vyenne
satte/ & wete ye wel that ful gracyously and curtoysly he 15
serued and kerued before hyr/

¶ *How Parys gate the prys of the Ioustes in the cyte of Vyenne/*

Whan the day was comen that the lordes knyghtes &
gentylmen shold Iuste for loue of the ladyes/ Parys
& Edward yede to a secrete place where they armed
them secretly and syn came to the lystes with theyr badges 20
& tokens and were horsed and armed ful rychely and wel/
Alle other knyghtes there were knowen by theyr armes/ but
the two whyte knyghtes were vnknowen/

The daulphyn thenne commaunded that euery one shold
mustre [a iij^v] or the Ioustyng began along the felde tofore 25
the ladyes & damoyselles/ and soo they mostred rydyng tofore
the scaffold of the fayre vyenne & were so nobly & rychely
armed & arayed/ and so godely men they were that euery one
sayd/ the floure of knyghthode may now be seen in thys place/
a emonge al other prynces Edward of Englond was moost 30
amerous of al & ryght renommed in armes/ The pucelle
Vyenne seyng alle these noble knyghtes/ sayd to hyr damoysel
ysabel/ Fayr syster whyche of them al thynke you that moost
dooth for the loue of me/ & ysabel ansuerd/ honourable lady

me semeth he that bereth the lyon of gold in his armes dooth
more for your loue than the other/ Certes sayd vyenne yonder
two whyt knyghtes that bere none armes in theyr sheldes are
more to my fantasye than ony of the other alwaye/ we shal
see now what they can doo/ Thenne were the knyghtes redy 5
to do fayte of armes/ And fyrst an hardy & valyaunte knyght
that bare in hys armes a crowne of gold bygan the fyrst cours/
& ayenst hym ranne the good knyght edward parys felowe &
recountred eche other so vygorously þᵗ they brake bothe theyr
speres/ many other mette eche other sodaynlye gyuyng grete 10
strokes/ somme were ouerthrowen to the erthe & somme brake
theyr speres worthely & kept theyr sterops ryght valyauntly/
the other recountred eche other so manfully that bothe hors
and man were caste to the grounde/ For euery man dyd hys
best to gete worshyp there/ Edward the kynges sone of 15
englond bare hym ful wel and had the better vpon many a
kny3t there/ but the strong kny3t parys broched hys hors
toward hym/ and mette hym so vygorously that atte ende he
ouerthrewe hym & had the better of hym wherof he gate grete
worshyp and was moche praysed for hys grete prowesse/ Thys 20
Ioustyng lasted tyl souper tyme/ & whan þᵉ euen cam many
of them were wery of the Iouste & rested them/ but parys
dyd thenne more of armes shewyng his meruayllous prowesse
than he had doon of al that day in so moche that none durst
approche hym ne withstonde his appertyse in armes/ & so 25
moche he dyd that thonour & prys of the Ioustes rested &
abode in hym that day/

¶ *How the shelde of crystal & the garlond with floures of gold*
were yeuen to Parys as to the best doer in faytes of armes/

The feste ended/ grete worshyp & loenge abode to þᵉ ij
kny3tes with þᵉ whyt [a iiijʳ] armes/ and Parys was ledde
vnto the scaffold there as vyenne was the whyche delyuerd 30
hym the shelde of crystal & the garlond wyth floures of gold
that she helde in hyr honde/ & thenne parys with Edward his
felawe departed thens in the secretest wyse that they coude

and wente to vnarme them to þe place where they fyrst armed
them self/ The barons and knyghtes that were there spake wel
of the prowesse & of the chyualrye of the knyghtes with the
whyt armes so that the daulphyn & the other grete lordes had
grete desyre to knowe what they were & to haue theyr 5
acqueyntaunce/ but they departed so secretly fro the felde
that no man knewe where they were become nor what waye
they toke

After al thys was thus doon the knyghtes retorned in to
theyr contrees spekyng euer of the ryal feste and chere that 10
the daulphyn had doon to them/ & of the prowesse of the
whyt knyghtes & of the ryght souerayn beaute and noblesse
of vyenne/ And in the mene whyle there moeued a stryf
betwyxte the barons & kny3tes of Frauunce and of Englond
For somme were there that were amerous of the doughter of 15
the duc of Normandye/ and somme were that loued and bare
oute the beaulte¹ of the syster of the kyng of Englond/ sayeng
she was fayrer than Vyenne was/ and other were there that
helde contrarye oppynyon sayeng that the daulphyns doughter
vyenne passed in beaute al other wymmen in the world/ and 20
for this reason was grete debate & stryf betwyxte the kny3tes
of fraunce & them of Englond for the beaute of these thre
damoyselles/

¶ Euer multeplyed & grewe more the bruyt and the renomme
of the daulphyn by cause of the Ioustes and tournoyment doon 25
in his cyte of vyenne/ wherof he had grete Ioye/ for they had
be moche honourable and playsaunt to al knyghtes/ And
Vyenne euer thought in hyr self who myght he be that had
goten the worshyp and prys of the Ioustes and sayd to ysabel/
Neuer truste me dere suster but þe kny3t to whom I haue 30
yeuen the shelde of crystal and my garlond is he that so
swetely sange for the loue of me tofore our chambre/ for myn
hert gyueth it me/ and by my fayth syster he is ful noble and
worthy/ & in alle hys dedes ryght curtoys and gentyl as we
myght haue seen whylere wherfor I say you my swete syster 35
that in hym I haue putte the rote of myn entyere herte/ my
wylle and al my loue/ nor neuer I shal haue playsyr ne Ioye

¹ bealute C.

[*Paris and Vienne*]

[a iiij^v] vnto þe tyme that I knowe what he is/ for my loue is al hys/ & of what so euer estate he be of I neuer shal take myn herte fro hym/ ¶ Thenne began she to wayle and syghe for the loue of hym ful tenderly/ for tyl now she had not felte the sparkles of loue that sprange out of hyr hert/ but parys knewe nothyng herof þt she desyred to haue hym & to knowe what he was/ but he kepte hys loue secrete in hys hert/ For he durst not shewe it vnto hyr wherfore he ledde hys lyf in grete trystesse and sorowe he went euer in the felawshyp of the bysshop of saynt Laurence & made semblaunte of nothyng And Iames the fader of Parys that had seen the noble feest and the ryal Ioustes in the cyte of vyenne/ wenyng to hym that hys sone parys had not ben there was ful sory & had grete dysplaysyr of it and sayd/ Fayr sone Parys I am in a grete malencolye & in a thought for you that ye be not so Ioyeful ne mery as ye were wonte to be/ here afore tyme I sawe you euer redy to the Ioustes and to al maner faytes of chyualrye for to gete honour/ & I now see you al chaunged syn ye took acqueyntaunce wyth thys bysshop for lothe I were to see you bycome a man of relygyon as I fere he wyl brynge you to/ and ryght wrothe I am that ye were not at that noble and ryal tournoyment that hath be holden in vyenne for the sake of alle the ladyes of thys londe/ wherfore dere sone I praye you to take hede to your self that ye lese not your good renommee/ your worshyp ne the praysyng also that ye gate afore tyme/ and that ye spende not your yongthe in ydlenesse/ And Parys heryng alle thys ansuerd noo thyng to hys fader but abode stylle pensyffull[1] thynkyng on þe beaute of vyenne/

Now sayth thystorye that as ye haue herde aboue a grete stryf befyl emong the knyghtes aforesayd for the loue of the thre damoyselles afore sayd/ For the erles sone of Flaundres was gretely wrothe for thys cause wyth the Duc of brennes and had beten & hurte sore eche other so that none myȝt make the pees betwyxte theym/ For eyther of hem mayntened & bare oute the beaute of his lady ¶ It happed

[1] pensyflull C.

[Paris and Vienne]

thenne that fyue knyghtes hardy and valyaunte came forth
the whyche sayd that they were redy to fyght and for to proue
by force of armes that Florye the dukes doughter of Normandye
was the fayrest damoysel of alle the world/ And Incontynent
stert vp fyue other knyghtes that said & mayntened [a v^r]
that constaunce the kynges syster of englond was the fayrest/
And forthwyth other v knyghtes rose vp that mayntened and
vphelde the beaute of vyenne aboue alle other wymmen in the
world in so moche that thys debate cam to the knowleche of
the kyng of Fraunce whiche sayd that herof myght growe a
grete trouble and dyscorde emong his barons & other lordes/
Soo sente he worde to them that they shold come toward hym
and that he shold gyue suche a sentence vpon theyr stryf that
they al shold be therof contente/ the whyche message plesed
them wel and came alle toward hym assone as they myght/
And whan they were come tofore the kyng they spake of theyr
stryf/ But anone the kyng ordeyned a Ioustes for the loue of
the sayd thre ladyes/ & made his maundement that they al
shold come wyth theyr armes and hors for to Iouste the viij
day of septembre in the cyte of parys/ and they that shold do
best in armes at that day they shold haue the prys & the
worshyp of the feste and the lady on whos beaute they helde
with shold be reputed and holden for the fayrest damoysel of
alle the world/ The kyng of Fraunce thenne sente worde to
the faders of the forsayd thre ladyes prayeng them to come
atte same feste and that eyther of them shold brynge wyth
hym a present of rychesse the which thre presentes shold be
yeuen in the worshyp of their thre doughters to the best doer
in armes in token of vyctorye/ And thus the kyng of englond
fyrst sent for hys syster Constaunce a fayre crowne of gold
alle sette wyth perlys and precyous stones of grete value/ The
duc of Normandye for loue of hys doughter Florye sente a
ryght fayre garlond sette wyth dyuers perlys & precyous stones
moche ryche and of grete extymacyon/ And the daulphyn for
loue of hys doughter[1] vyenne sente a moche ryche coler of
gold al enuyronned wyth precyous stones of dyuers colours/
the whiche was worth a ryght grete tresour/ And these thre

[1] doughrer C.

Iewellys were delyuerd to the kynge of Fraunce/ The forsayd
knyghtes thenne made them redy and apparaylled al thynges
accordyng to the Ioustes/ & in ryche araye came al to the
cyte of Parys/ and wete ye wel that in Fraunce was not seen
afore that day so grete noblesse of barons and knyghtes as 5
were there assembled/ for there were the moost hye prynces
& barons of englond of Fraunce and of Normandye and eyther
of them dyd sette al hys wytte and entendement to vpholde
and bere oute that they [a v^v] had purposed and sayd/ and
euery baron gaf hys lyuerey that they shold be knowen eche 10
fro other/ & the bruyt & renomme was that my lady constaunce
shold haue thonour of that feste for thys that many a fayre
and hardy knyght made them redy to mayntene the quarelle
of hyr beaulte/ but neuertheles eyther of these thre partyes
hoped to haue the worshyp of the feste/ & parys that was in 15
vyenne the cyte/ and that wel knewe the grete apparaylle of
thys feste/ took counceyl of Edward hys felawe whether he
shold goo to parys or not/ And Edward counceylled hym to
goo thyder/ so that he wente secretly/ & sayd yf ye goo thyder
secretly and yf god gyue you grace that ye gete the worshyp 20
of the feste/ grete wele & good shal come to you therby/ and
yf ye goo and be knowen the daulphyn and the other lordes
shal not preyse you soo moche as they shold yf ye were
vnknowen for cause that ye be not of so grete lygnage as they
be/ another is yf ye goo openly and that my lady vyenne 25
happeth to haue thonour of the feste by your prowesse/ she
shal nought be sette by/ consyderyng the other grete lordes
that shal be there procedyng your degree/ & yf she gete the
worshyp of the feste by a knyght vnknowen the loue and
honour shal growe the more in hyr courage toward hym that 30
thus hath doon for hyr sake/ wherfore I counceyl you to goo
thyder in the moost secretest wyse that ye may/ for my truste
is that ye shal gete grete worshyp there/ and but yf ye goo/
truste me I shal make my self redy to goo thyder for you/ For
I wyl be lothe to see the beaulte of my lady vyenne to be 35
rebuked At these wordes graunted Parys to goo to the sayd
Ioustes/ and whan he was redy & had al thynges accordyng
to a noble knyght he departed in the secretest manere that

[Paris and Vienne] 13

he myght toward the cyte of parys where as the kyng of
Fraunce maad grete prouysyon of alle maner metes and of al
other thynges necessarye to suche a ryal feste/ And in the
myddes of the cyte of parys he ordeyned the place where the
knyghtes shold Iouste and dyd doo make many fayre scaffoldes 5
for the ladyes and damoyselles to be sette on/ for to beholde
the Ioustyng/ Also he dyd do make thre baners ful fayre and
ryche/ the fyrst baner was whyt/ and there was wryton vpon
hit in letters of gold/ vyenne doughter to my lord godfroy of
alenson daulphyn of vyennoys/ the second baner was rede/ 10
and was wryton theron in letters of gold/ Constaunce the
[a vj^r] kynges syster of englond/ The thyrd baner was whyt
and in letters of gold was wryton theron/ Florye doughter to
the duc of normandye/ and these iij baners were pyght vp at
the thre corners[1] of the felde/ and wete ye that so grete prees 15
was there that the peple took theyr place vpon the scaffoldes
ij dayes afore the feste for to see the grete peple & the fayr
ordynaunce that there was/

Whan it was so that the lordes were redy of alle thynges
that were necessarye/ and were departed fro theyr 20
contrees they assembled al at parys the xiiij day of
septembre/ and neuer tofore was seen so grete a companye of
nobles/ For fro alle partyes was comen grete chyualrye/ the
somme for to do armes/ and the other for to see the feste
whyche was moche sumptuous and noble/ & whan the day 25
assygned came of the Ioustes/ On the mornyng erly he dyd
doo sette these thre Ioyaulx or Iewels in the baners/ the
whyche shone and resplendysshed moche merueillously for the
nombre of perles & precyous stones that were in the baners/
Now it shold be ouerlonge to recyte of the barons and of the 30
knyghtes that were in that Iourneye/ For many were comen
thyder fro the royame of spayne/ of aragon and of many other
contrees for to proue their strengthe and persones/ and for
to mayntene the barons that mayntened the thre ladyes
maydens/ Of whome we shall reherce of the pryncypallest 35
here after the shortest wyse we may/ And whan it came in
the mornyng that euery man was armed & apparaylled in the

[1] cornes C.

felde/ and that the kyng of Fraunce was sette in hys grete[1]
scaffolde/ and began to say al alowde and moche meruayllously/
that alle the people myght here and vnderstonde/ Knyghtes
and barons that been here for to do the fayte of armes goo ye
eueryche vnder that baner that he wyl mayntene for the loue 5
of hys lady/ and we gyue in comaundement that this felde be
of loue and of curtosye/ as it to you apperteyneth/ how be it
we wyl wel that eche of you do valyantly hys armes and hys
chyualryes for that damoysell whyche he wyl mayntene/ And
he that shal wynne the felde shal haue the prys and thonour 10
of the feste/ and that lady or damoysel shal be mayntened
and allowed for the moost fayre damoysel of the world/ and
shal haue the prys and thonour of them of Englond of Fraunce
& of Normandye/ and that to thys noo man be so hardy to
gaynsay vpon the payne to lose his lyf [a vj^v]/ And yet after 15
thys he sayd/ ye see here a fayre crowne the whyche the quene
of Fraunce hath ordeyned/ to thende that it be delyuerd to
the fader of the damoysel that shal haue the prys and honour
of the felde and of the Ioustes/ And the knyght that shal gete
the prys and thonour of the Ioustes shal haue all the thre 20
baners and the thre Iewels that been in them/ & comaunded
that the baner of Normandye shold fyrst make hys mustre/ &
nexte the baner of Constaunce and thenne that of Vyenne/

¶ And fyrst vnder the baner of Normandye were they that
folowe/ that is to wete Iohan sone of therle of Flaunders/ 25
Phelyp of bauyers neuew of the kynge of Fraunce/ Edward
sone of the duke of bourgoyne/ Iohan erle of Armynak/ Balaxe
brother of the marquys of Saluce Geffroy duc of pycardye/
And after them came many other wel armed & habylled/ After
came the baner of Constaunce/ the whiche accompanyed Iohan 30
sone of the duc of bremeos/ Gastamons of gastre brother of
the erle of foyes/ Anthonye alegre sone of the duc of Carnes/
Larer neuew of the duc of bourgoyne/ The honourable Iohan
of braban/ Salamon de launson brother of therle of the marche/
and after them came many other barons and knyghtes/ and 35
thenne after came the baner of the fayr vyenne/ the whyche
accompanyed hughe sone of the duc of Bourbon/ Edward sone

[1] hrete C.

[Paris and Vienne] 15

of the kyng of Englond/ Wylliam sone of the duc of barry/
Antonye sone of the counte of prouynce/ Parys sone of syr
Iaques of vyenne/ Dormando of monferrant sone of the
marquys/ thre sones of the duc of Carnes/ Iohan peryllous
duc of Normandye/ & after them came many other barons 5
and knyghtes wel armed & wel horsed/ And whan the mustre
was made/ euery baner retorned in to hys place/ whyche
moche noble and meruayllous thynge was it to see and to
byholde the noblesse of the barons & knyghtes soo wel horsed
and armed as they were/ And the daulphyn and syr Iaques 10
fader of Parys were comen for to see the feste & the Ioustes/

¶ *How Parys wan the prys at the Ioustes in the cyte of Parys/*

Whan thenne it came to the hour of tyerce began the
Ioustes/ and cam in to the felde moche nobly armed
Iohan sone of therle of flaundres/ & ageyn hym came
Iohan sone of the duke of brennes & coped to gyder so fyersly 15
þt they [a vijʳ] brake theyr speres/ and Iohan sone of therle of
flaunders tombled to therthe vnder hys hors/ & after ayenst
Iohan de brennes came Edward sone of the duke of bourgoyne/
These ij knyghtes bete down puyssauntly Iohan de brennes/
vnto the tyme þt there came ayenst hym Iohan peryllous duc 20
of Normandye/ whyche smote hym wyth soo grete force that
he ouerthrewe hym vnder hys hors & brake hys arme & put
hym in suche estate that he wyst not whether it was day or
nyght/ and ayenst Iohan peryllous came Anthonye alegre sone
of the duc of carnes/ and dyd so moche prowesse wyth his 25
persone that he conquerd Iohan peryllous and v other knyghtes
myghty men of his partye whom he smote to the erthe by
force of armes/ After came ageynst anthonie alegre Geffroy
of pycardye and smote anthonie in suche wyse that he fyl to
the erthe/ & vj other stronge knyghtes of hys partye/ and 30
after dyd soo meruayllous feates of armes/ that euery man
sayd that he had thonour of the felde/ And thenne came the
free knyght parys ayenst geffroy beryng lowe hys spere/ &
they gaf so grete strokes that the knyghtes and horses wente

16   [*Paris and Vienne*]

al to therthe/ wherfor the kyng sayd/ that sythe bothe two
were throwen to the erthe/ that they shold retorne ageyn to
the Ioustes/ & parys wyth a grete desyre consented/ and soo
bothe retorned & came rennyng/ And Parys gaf to geffroy so
grete a stroke/ that hys hors slode and thenne geffroy ouer- 5
threwe to the erthe/ but by cause that the hors slode it
was sayd that the hors was cause that he ouerthrewe/ For
moche they mayntened geffroy and sayd that he was not
vaynquysshed/ & that it shold be wel doon that they shold
Iuste ageyn/ And by cause that Parys was not knowen ther 10
was none that mayntened hym ne susteyned/ neuertheles the
kyng of fraunce knewe wel that geffroy was vaynquysshed
loyally & wel/ For he had wel seen the aduenture/ & wold do
no wronge vnto the knyght whyche was of grete strengthe and
myght/ and anone sente to hym an heraulde whyche sayd to 15
hym in the name of the kynge of fraunce/ that the kyng had
wel seen & wel knewe that Parys had vaynquysshed hys
knyght/ Notwythstondyng yf he wold yet ones retorne to the
Iuste by hys noblesse that he shold do hym self grete honour
And thenne Parys maad hys ansuer sayeng that the beaulte 20
of my lady vyenne was so grete that in al the world was none
to hyr lyke/ that yf it pleased the Kyng I am redy for to
[a vij^v] furnysshe the Ioustes for hys loue ayenst the knyght
yet another tyme/ and to Iuste tyl that geffroy shold be
vaynquysshed/ & that was wythoute ony gaynsayeng/ & the 25
heraulde retorned and tolde it to the kyng/ wherof the kyng
was wel contente & sayd that the knyght ought to be somme
grete lord/ For he was of grete valoyr and puyssaunce and
spake moche swetely and curtoysly/ And after Parys chaunged
and took another hors/ whyche Edward hys felowe had made 30
redy for hym & retorned to the Iustes/ & smote to gyder wyth
soo grete myght/ that by veray force geffroy went to therthe
vnder hys hors ryght euyl hurte/

Thenne whan it came toward euen the Ioustes were so
grete thycke and stronge that al the thre partyes as wel 35
of one as of other were throwen doun to the erthe/ that
there abode no moo of the partye of vyenne but parys allone/

and of the partye of normandye thre knyghtes stronge and
puyssaunt and they were Balaxo brother of the marquys of
Saluces/ Iohan sone of the erle of Armynack/ and phelyp of
bauyere/ & of the partye of constaunce other thre stronge &
myghty/ that is to wete Iohan of braband/ larer neuew of the
duc of bourgeyn/ and Salamon dalanson brother of þe counte
de la marche and they sayd that the Iustes shold abyde tyl
on the morne/ for they were moche wery/ and whan parys
saw that they wold haue retorned/ he fewtred hys spere/ and
there cam ayenst hym balaxo brother of the marquys of
saluces/ And Parys at the fyrst stroke strake hym doun to
the erthe vnder hys hors/ and in lyke wyse dyd to the other
v/ and moche nobly & valyauntly he wanne thonour of the
Iustes and of the felde/

¶ *How the kyng commaunded that the thre baners wyth the iij
Iewellys shold be gyuen to Parys champyon of vyenne/*

The Ioustes fynysshed Parys wanne the beaute of hys
lady the fayre vyenne/ and he was ledde to the scaffolde
where as the kynge was/ & the other grete lordes &
knyghtes & there were delyuerd to hym the thre baners & the
thre Iewellys that were in them/ & Parys shewed them thurgh
all the felde/ in sygne that the sayd vyenne had goten thonour
for to be the fayrest damoysell that was in alle the world by
the same yonge knyght/ and whan Parys had the thre fayr
baners and the thre ryche Iewellys/ he [a viij^r] and Edward hys
felowe departed out of the cyte of parys and oute of fraunce
the moost secrete wyse that they myght/ & retorned in to
dalphyne/ Parys retorned in to the companye of the forsayd
bysshop of Saynt Laurence/ as he had not been at the feste/ &
alwaye he demaunded tydynges of the Iustes that were made
in fraunce/ and who had thonour of the Ioustes/

Whan the feste was made al the barons & knyghtes that
were there had grete desyre to knowe who was he that
so valyauntly & so nobly had wonne the Iourneye &
the honour of the Iustes for to doo to hym worshyp/ but they

coude neuer knowe hym/ wherof they had grete dysplaysyr/ & sayd that the knyght was of grete wysedom/ by cause he wold not be knowen/ And after this the barons & knyghtes took leue of the kyng/ and retorned in to theyr londes al dyscomforted/ by cause they had not goten the honour of the feste/ and yet were they more angry by cause they knewe not to whome the honour was gyuen of the feste ne of the Iustes/ The kyng of Fraunce whyche moche loued the dolphyn made to hym grete feste & moche grete honour/ And the kyng delyuerd to hym the crowne that the quene had gyuen/ for to gyue to hyr that shold haue the honour of the Ioustes/ to thende that he shold gyue it vnto hys doughter vyenne in sygne & token that she was the moost fayr damoysel of the world/ & whan al thys was doon/ the dolphyn and the fader of parys retorned in to dolphyne in moche grete honour and grete[1] Ioye/ whan vyenne knewe that hyr fader came she came and mette hym as she was accustomed/ Thenne whan the dolphyn sawe hyr/ he kyssed hyr & sette on her hede the crowne whyche the kynge had gyuen hym/ and tolde to hyr how she had goton the honour for to be the moost fayrest damoysell of the world/ and loo here is the fayr crowne that the quene of fraunce sendeth to you in token that ye haue goten the honour/ Notwythstondyng fayr doughter/ that ye haue had many contrarye therto/ but ye haue had a good deffendour & ry3t stronge and hath wel quyted hym in your nede/ For of eche partye were abyden thre knyghtes moche stronge and puyssaunte/ and on your partye was left but one knyght onely whyche vaynquysshed al the other/ wythout ony token/ and is departed alle secretly that no man knewe hym ne the kyng of fraunce hath no knowleche of hym/ but he hath [a viij v] borne awaye wyth hym the thre baners & the iij Iewellys that were in them & also the prys & thonour of the feste/ wherfore swete & fayr doughter ye wote neuer to whom to gyue thankynges of so moche honour as hath be doon for you/ but I praye to god of heuen & to the glorious vyrgyn marye/ that it playse hym to gyue to hym good & honour/ Ioye & excellence & in alle his feates vyctorye/ lyke as he is

[1] grere C.

[Paris and Vienne]

chyef & hede of al honour and of al chyualrye in thys world
For I neuer sawe ne herde of knyght that so gracyously and
so curtoysly bare hym in his armes & in his chyualryes/ And
whan vyenne herde speke of these tydynges/ & sawe the grete
honour & prys that she had goten and al was comen by this 5
noble knyght/ she sayd to ysabeau hyr damoysel/ My suster
sayd I not to you wel but late/ that I was byloued by the
moost noble and valyaunt knyght of fraunce/ & by my fayth
my swete suster/ this is he þ^t so swetely songe & that wanne
the Iustes in this cyte & bare with hym the shelde of crystal 10
& my garlonde/ and went his waye so that noo man myght
knowe hym/ aduyse you wel fayr suster what honour is comen
to me by his prowesse & by his bounte/ I may wel be sory
& dolant/ whan I may not knowe who he is/ & myn herte is
moche heuy & myn entendement that I neuer can fynde the 15
moyen to see & knowe hym/ and yet she sayd/ Certes my
swete suster ysabeau/ I byleue that my dayes be shorte/ &
that I shall deye of somme cruel & fals deth for the grete
desplaysyr that I haue contynuelly in my herte/ for I can none
other thynge doo but wepe & waylle/ & alwaye to contynue 20
in sorouful lyf & heuy but none apperceyued it but onely hyr
damoysel ysabeau/

The fader of parys whyche had ben with the dolphyn in
that feste had not seen there hys sone Parys/ wherof he
had grete sorowe in his herte/ for he had seen that he 25
was accustomed to be in al noble Iustes/ but thenne he sawe
hym goo with the bysshop of saynt Laurence/ and dysposed
hym not to doo armes as he was woned/ wherfor he sayd to
hym on a day My sone I had hoped to haue had in the grete
consolacyon/ but now thou bryngest[1] me in to grete heuynesse 30
and dysplaysyr/ whan I see that thou wylt not departe from
thys bysshop wherfor I praye the that þ^u leue hym/ & doo
soo that it may be to me playsaunt and to the honneste/
Parys herde hym wel/ but he gaf not a word to ansuer [b j^r]
The fader of Parys seyng thys went to his secrete felowe 35
Edward and sayd to hym/ I see wel that the grete amytye

[1] byngest C.

& loue that ye haue to my sone/ and knowe ye for certayn
that I haue in my hert grete melancolye whan I remembre
that Parys hath had grete honour & fame of chyualrye/ and
now I see that he gooth al wyth thys bysshop/ and leteth hys
hawkes/ his houndes and hors to deye for hongre/ wherfore 5
I praye you that ye wyl gyue me somme counceyl/ whyche
am soo meschaunt that I deye for sorowe/ And whan he had
sayd these wordes/ Edward had pyte of hym/ & comforted
hym the beste wyse he coude/ and departed fro hym/ and
wente strayte to hys felowe Parys and sayd to hym I knowe 10
wel that loue constrayneth the so strongely/ that thou hast
noo power ouer thy self/ wherfore thy lyf may not longe
endure/ And also thy fader and thy frendes ben euyl contente
ayenst the/ and I say to the that for to be vertuous and
valyaunt it playseth moche to god/ And for the loue of one 15
woman thou doost moche desplaysyr to thy fader/ And also
for noo persone what someuer he or she be/ thou oughtest not
to lese the wele & renomee that thou hast of chyualrye/ It
appyereth not in the/ that thou hast ony vertu or courage/
wherfore I praye the that thou wylt do somme thyng that it 20
may be playsaunt to thy fader whych hath desyred & prayed
me that I shold soo say to the/ whan parys had herde al this/ he
ansuerd to edward and sayd to hym/ I knowe wel that these
thynges that thou hast sayd to me been vertuous & honnest/
but they been to me greuous/ for to put me from the thoughtes 25
in whyche I am contynuelly/ Neuertheles I praye the that thou
gyue me counceyl what is beste that I doo/ Thenne sayd
edward it shold wel playse me/ yf it were thy playsyr that we
shold goo in to braband/ For it is vj monethes passed that
I haue not seen my lady/ & there shall we do armes/ by which 30
we may gete fame and honour/ & paris agreed therto sayeng
that he was contente yf it playsed hym so to do/ & Incontynent
they made redy theyr harnoys & horses and alle thynges
necessarye to them/ & or Parys departed he put in hys
chambre al the thynges & pryses that he had wonne by 35
chyualryes & closed them fast in his chambre/ & delyuerd
the keye to his moder & prayed hir moche derly that she
shold not open it/ ne suffre þ^t ony persone shold entre therin/

And after they wente toward Braband/ where as they dyd grete [b j^v] feates of chyualrye & Ioustes wherof they gate grete honoure and worshyp/ and were moche praysed of ladyes and damoysellys/ And parys made countenaunce for to haue abyden in braband for the loue of edward but hys hert drewe vnto the fayre Vyenne/ whome he so moche loued in hys herte secretely/

¶ *How Dyane and vyenne hyr doughter wenten to vysyte the fader of Parys the whyche was seek/*

Now it happened that duryng thys tyme that Parys and Edward duelleden in Braband/ the fader of Parys fyl in to a sekenesse of feures or accesse/ And the cause came of the thought that he had of hys sone Parys/ And he beyng seek the doulphyn wente on a day to see hym/ and demaunded the cause of hys maladye/ and comforted hym the best wyse that he coude/ and after retorned home/ and sayd to hys wyf/ that it were wel doon that she shold goo see and vysyte messyre Iaques whyche was seke/ And forthwyth Incontynent my lady dyane/ hyr doughter Vyenne and ysabeau hyr damoysel wyth a grete companye went to the castel of Syr Iaques/ and salewed hym moche nobly as it wel apperteyned/ & the best wyse that they myght ¶ And whan they were in the chambre where messyre Iaques was and laye/ Dame dyane demaunded hym of his sekenesse And messire Iaques sayd that al hys dysease came for hys sone Parys/ by cause he loste so hys tyme/ and that he went alway wyth the bysshop of Saynt laurence/ wherof I fere me that he shal become a man of relygyon/ I haue no moo chyldren but hym/ I wote not what I shall doo wyth the goodes that god hath gyuen to me/ And my lady dyane comforted hym and sayd that hys sone was moche wel byloued of the doulphyn/ & that he had moche grete amytye of many grete lordes/ barons & knyghtes/ & also she sayd that emong al thynges he shold ordeyne for hys helthe/ & after all thys the moder of parys prayed hyr that it myght playse hyr to come see the castel/

and she ansuerd that she moche desyred it Thenne the moder
of parys shewed hir al the castel/ & ledde hir in to an halle
al ful of armes and abylemens of warre for to fyght in batayll/
After she ladde hyr in to another[1] halle where as were many
hawkes/ faulcens/ and many other fowles of chace/ And after 5
in to many [b ij^r] other halles & chambres rychely arayed
whyche were ouer longe to reherce/ And after the moder of
Parys shewed vnto hyr the chambre of Parys where that he
slepte/ wherin were many abylments/ whyche shold wel
suffyse þe chambre of a grete prynce And in the sayd chambre 10
were two grete standardes couerd after the guyse of Fraunce/
That one was ful of clothe of gold and sylke/ and that other
of harnoys and of many other thynges/ Thenne sayd Vyenne
to ysabeau/ by my fayth fayr syster I haue noo grete meruaylle
of thys yonge knyght Parys though of hym be maad grete 15
mencyon/ For thordynaunce of thyse thynges shewe wel that
he is of grete valure/ And in byholdyng of these thynges she
sawe a couerture of an hors alle whyte/ And hyr semed that
it was the same that the knyght bare that wanne the prys of
the Ioustes that was made in the cyte of Vyenne/ and that 20
had the shelde of crystal & the garlond whych she tolde to
ysabeau And ysabeau ansuerd to hyr/ neuer thynke ye soo/
For all day been made semblable[2] couertures and tokenes
whyte/ wherof ye may wel be deceyued/ Vyenne enforced alle
waye hyr self to take[3] better hede/ and of the grete Ioye that 25
she had she sayd to hyr moder/ Madame I am a lytel crased
and sodeynly taken/ wherfore yf it playse you I wold fayne
reste a lytel in this chambre/ and late me be alle allone wyth
my suster ysabeau/ for I wyl haue none other/ and anone eche
body auoyded oute of the chambre/ and ysabeau dyd shytte 30
the dore that none myght come in/ ¶Thenne sayd vyenne
now we shal see yf we may fynde ony thynge that we may
haue better knowleche of/ For myn herte sayth yes/ After
that they had serched and vysyted alle the chambre/ they
cam on a syde of the chambre where they fonde a lytel dore/ 35
of whyche henge a lytel keye by a thwonge/ and anone they
opened the dore and entred therin And there was a lytel

[1] anothrr C.   [2] semalable C.   [3] tuke C.

chambre whyche was xij foot longe/ and was an oratorye/
where as was the mageste of our Lord Ihesu Cryst vpon a lytel
aulter and at eche corner was a canstyke of syluer/ and
thyder cam Parys for to make hys sacrefyse whan he aroos/
and whan he wente to hys bedde/ 5
¶ And there were the thre baners that the noble knyght
Parys had wonne in the cyte of Parys/ And the thre Iewellys
of the thre damoyselles aforesayd/ And in the same place was
also the shelde of Crystal [b ij^v] and the garlond that Vyenne
delyuerd to hym whan he wanne the prys at the Ioustes in 10
the cyte of vyenne/ And all these he kepte secrete in that
place/ And whan vyenne sawe these thynges/ she was sure
that Parys was he whome she had so moche desyred to knowe/
and that soo moche honour had doon to hyr/ and for the grete
Ioye that she had/ she sette hyr doun on the grounde/ and 15
there abode a grete whyle/ and coude not speke a word/ And
after she spake to ysabeau/ & sayd my swete syster/ blessyd
and preysed be our lord of thys good Iourney/ For me thynketh
I shold neuer departe oute of thys chambre/ Alas I haue so
longe abyden to knowe/ who he was that so swetely played in 20
his Instrumentes so nygh vnto me/ and now he is so ferre/ &
thenne ysabeau began to repreue hyr and sayd to hyr/ Swete
lady I praye you that ye say ne do ony thyng whiche myght
torne you to folye/ and be ye ruled by wysedom and reason/
For not wythstondyng that parys haue so moche good & 25
vertues/ yet ye ought to consyder that he is not egal to you
in lygnage ne in estate/ For I knowe wel that many noble
& puyssaunt lordes haue demaunded you in maryage/ & loue
you & do grete thynges for you/ and also thonour of Parys
whyche is your vayssal and subget is not egall ne worthy vnto 30
you/ ¶ Thenne vyenne was moche angry on ysabeau and began
to say/ A veray god I am wel dyscomforted and deceyued by
the/ that thus agaynsayest me of hym that I so longe haue
desyred to knowe/ Alas I had supposed that in noo thyng ye
wold haue dysplaysed me/ And in good fayth I say to the/ 35
that this man I wyl loue and demaunde/ and I promyse the
in good fayth/ that yf thou ony more gaynsaye me I shal slee
my self/ and thenne thou shalt be cause of my deth/ For I wyl

not lese hym that I haue so longe loued/ but I say to the for trouthe/ that yf thou euer say to me suche wordes of my frende parys/ that thou shalt neuer after haue space to say them ageyn another tyme/ for yf thou consyderest wel hys noble condycyons and custommes/ thou sholdest preyse hym 5 better than thou doost/ And knowest thou not wel that the kyng of fraunce wold that it had coste hym half hys Royame that hys sone Lowys were as valyaunte as parys is/ ¶And also there be many notable lordes that desyre to knowe his name/ and to haue hys amytye/ 10

¶Thenne take hede and byholde by my fayth yf euer thou sawe [biij^r] man that myght be compared to hym/ certaynly alle vertues been in hym/ And sythe that fortune hath brought me to hys loue/ he is worthy to haue my loue/ and yet more than is in me/ And haue I not reason & cause thenne to loue 15 hym/ whyche hath doon to me so grete good and honour and doubtyng noo peryl of hys persone/ and is it not wel grete worshyp to my fader to haue for vaissal and subget the beste knyght that is in all the world For in alle the world is noo knyght that I wold forsake parys fore/ ne oone that hath 20 doon so moche for me/ And thus to speke of the feates of Parys she coude[1] not stynte/

¶Thenne came two damoyselles knockyng at the chambre dore sayeng/ Vyenne ye must come to my lady/ And ysabeau sprange oute sayeng that she shold come anone/ And vyenne 25 seyng that she must nedes departe fro thens sayd to ysabeau/ My suster syth we must departe hens late vs take somme of these Iewellys/ and we shal kepe them secretly tyl that Parys[2] be comen and we shal see what countenaunce he shal make in hym self ¶Thenne they took the colyer and the whyte baner 30 of vyenne and other Iewellys and hydde them vnder theyr clothes/ and wente in to the chambre of messyre Iaques/ but vyenne desyred gretely to speke with paris and thought longe or he came home/ And in the mene whyle messire Iaques recouerd of his maladye and bycam alle hool wherof Vyenne 35 had grete Ioye but she durst not shewe it/

[1] doude C.   [2] Ptrys C.

¶ How Parys and Edward retorned oute of braband/

After certeyn tyme that Parys had be in Braband wyth hys felowe Edward/ he desyred strongely to see the fayr vyenne/ For the loue of hyr destrayned hym moche strongly/ ¶Neuertheles he durst not telle it to hys felowe/ to thende that he shold take noo dysplaysyr of hys departyng/ And sone after the space of v dayes Parys receyued a letter that hys fader was seek/ & thenne he sayd to Edward/ Ryght dere brother & felowe/ pleseth it you to wete that my fader is sore seke/ & me semeth it were good that we departed yf ye consente but I praye you that ye take noo desplaysyr¹ in thys departyng/ for yf it playse god we shal sone retorne/ And edward seyng the Iuste reason of Parys and hys good wylle/ sayd to hym that he was wel content & plesyd/ wherfore Incontynente they departed oute of braband [biij^v] and came in to the cyte of vyenne/ of whos comyng messyr Iaques had souerayn playsyr specyally/ by cause he had herde that Parys hys sone had doon valyauntly feates of armes/ ¶Now it happed that when Parys was arryued at home wyth hys fader lyke as he was accustomed/ Allewaye tofore or he wente to hys bedde/ he wente to make hys orysons and prayers/ and after he aduysed yf he lacked ony thynge/ and fonde that tho thynges that he loued beste were taken awaye/ wherof he was moche angry/ and quasi half in despayr in suche wyse that alle the nyght he coude not slepe And whan it came in the mornyng he came to hys moder and sayd/ Moder how is it that ye haue not kepte my chambre cloos and shytte/ For I lacke certayn thynges whyche I wold not gladly lese/ and haue for them grete dysplaysir/ To whom hys moder ansuerd/ My sone by my fayth there neuer entred therin persone/ but on a tyme whan your fader was seek came my lady dyane and hyr doughter vyenne/ and whan they had vysyted your fader/ they wente al aboute for to see thys castel/ and thenne they entred in to your chambre/ But I can not thynke that they took ony thyng for they taryed not longe/ sauf onely vyenne whyche taryed onely allone sauf hyr damoysel/ by cause she

---
¹ desplayryr C.

was euyl at ease at hyr hert/ wherfore my sone I praye you
to take noo dysplaysyr/ And thenne Parys sayd to hym self/ yf
none other theef haue taken it sauf she I shal not be dyscouerd/
Neuertheles I wote neuer yf Vyenne hath taken it awaye for
ony thynge/ ¶And after he arayed hym self and cladde hym 5
moche nobly/ & wente to do the reuerence to the daulphyn/
and to dame Dyane/ And after to Vyenne theyr doughter/ And
the dolphyn receyued hym moche curtoysly/ ¶And the
daulphyn demaunded hym tydynges and of many other
thynges/ 10
¶And whan the fayre lady Vyenne sawe parys of the grete
desyre that she had to see hym/ and of the grete loue that she
bare to hym/ alle hyr chere was coloured lyke a fresshe rose
in the monthe of Maye/ and coude not be contente ne fylled
to beholde hyr fayre loue and frende Parys/ And the more she 15
byhelde hym/ the more grewe and encreaced hyr loue toward
hym ¶And Parys beyng tofore the dolphyn on his knee moche
humbly durst not loke on Vyenne/ But in hys herte he had
grete payne/ And who had wel byholden hym/ had wel seen
in his [biiij^r] vysage hys thought/ And after that the dolphyn 20
had demaunded hym of that it plased hym Parys took leue
of the dolphyn and of my lady dyane & of vyenne theyr
doughter & retorned home to hys faders hous/

After a fewe dayes Vyenne in suche wyse as loue
destrayned hyr said to hyr damoysel ysabeau/ my 25
suster knowe ye for trouth that me semeth that parys
is moche pensyf/ and I byleue that it is for hys thynges
whyche he fyndeth not in his oratorye/ me semeth it is beste
that we lete hym haue knowleche that we haue them/ Isabeau
ansuerd/ it were wel doon soo/ but that it be doon honestly 30
and secretely/ Thenne sayd vyenne I shal aduyse the manere
After certeyn dayes vyenne sayd to hyr moder/ Madame I lete
you wete that I am a lytel charged in my conscyence/ & I
wold fayn confesse me to somme good persone/ And it is tolde
me that the bysshop of saynt laurence is a moche honest man 35
& deuoute/ wherfore madame I praye you to sende for hym
þt I myght speke wyth hym/ And my lady dyane seyng the

[Paris and Vienne] 27

good wylle of hyr doughter sente for to fetche the bysshop/
And vyenne confessyd hyr to hym moche deuoutely spekyng
alwaye of our lord & of hys commaundementes/ & after that
she was confessyd/ she prayed þe bysshop that he wold come
ageyn on the morne/ for she fonde grete comforte in his 5
wordes/ & that she wold telle hym somme thynges in grete
secrete/ And on the morne the bysshop came ageyn to vyenne/
& vyenne sayd to hym thus/ My ghoostly fader somme thynges
haue been taken away in a place/ the whiche longen to parys
sone of messyre Iaques/ And the persone that hath them hath 10
therof conscyence/ And therfore I praye you as moche as I
may/ that by your benygnyte ye say to hym that yf he may/
he come to morne hyther wyth you/ & the bysshop whyche
aduysed hym noo thyng of thentencyon and thought of vyenne
said that he shold brynge hym wythoute faute/ 15

¶ How vyenne dyscouuerd hyr courage to Parys

On the morne the bysshop came moche dylygently &
brought parys wyth hym/ And vyenne salewed parys
wythoute to make ony semblaunte of loue/ and parys
rendred hys salewes ageyn moche humbly/ And thenne Vyenne
wythdrewe hyr fro the bysshop and the other/ and said to 20
parys It is not longe sythe ye were [b iiij^v] goon in to braband/
and that I accompanyed my lady my moder for to goo vysyte
your fader whyche thenne was seek/ & we sawe and byhelde
al the castel vntyl we came to your oratorye & there I sawe
certayn Iewellys whyche moche wel pleased me and I took 25
them & haue kepte them vntyl thys present tyme/ And I shal
now rendre them to you ageyn/ & therfor I praye you that yf
I haue doon ony dysplaysyr or maad ony defaulte that ye
wyl pardonne me/ for I promyse to you by my fayth that
I haue doon it for none euyl/ To whome parys answerd humbly 30
and wyth grete reuerence & sayd moche curtoysly/ Madame
by your curtosye ye came to vysyte my fader/ of whyche
vysytacyon not onely my fader/ but alle our frendes haue
receyued grete & souerayn honour/ wherfore myn excellent

lady/ my fader/ my moder/ and I been alle youres/ and alle
that we haue also/ And yf by aduenture your ladyshyp had
ony playsyr to take of my Iewellys/ I ensure you by my
fayth/ that myn hert hath therin moche gretter playsyr than
hert of man may thynke and yet more shold haue yf the sayd 5
Iewellys were better the half than they be/ Soo thenne I praye
you ryght honourable damoysel that ye wyl pardonne me For
not al onely these Iewelles whyche been of lytel valewe but
my fader my moder and I been al youres/ and al redy to obeye
to your seruyce/ and knowe ye verayly that it is not longe 10
sythen/ that the sayd Iewels were by a frensshe knyght gyuen
to me/

Thenne sayd Vyenne ye nede not to say to me fro whens
these Iewels ben comen/ For I knowe them as wel as
ye/ And vyenne sayd/ I meruaylle me gretely how ye 15
so longe haue hydde your loue fro me/ I praye you as moche
as I may/ and by the fayth that ye haue toward me that ye
say to me the trouthe of that whyche I shal demaunde you/
for moche I desyre it to knowe/ ¶ Thenne sayd Parys ryght
honourable damoysel/ ye ought not to praye me/ where ye 20
haue power to commaunde me/ For alle that/ your ladyshyp
shal plese to demaunde me/ I shal say to you the trouth wyth
good hert & good wylle/ Thenne sayd vyenne I wyl fyrst that
ye say the trouthe/ that yf ye were he/ that in suche a yere
cam euery nyght syngyng and sownyng Instrumentes so 25
swetely tofore my chambre/ After I wyl that ye telle me yf
ye wanne the Iustes that were made the fyrst day of may in
this cyte/ And yf ye bare awaye the [b v^r] shelde of crystal
and the chapelet whyche I haue seen in your oratorye/ After
I wyl that ye say to me/ yf ye wanne the Iustes the xviij day 30
of septembre whyche were made in the cyte of parys/ where
as were so many noble knyghtes & barons/ & yf ye had goten
there the iij baners whyche I haue seen in your oratorye/ &
I praye you that ye telle to me/ yf ye haue doon to me suche
seruyce/ for suche thynges ye ought not to hyde/ And yf by 35
aduenture ye haue doon them for the loue of my fader or of
hys courte/ we be moche holden to you & be bounden to

[Paris and Vienne]

thanke you/ And yf by aduenture for ony lady or for the loue
of me ye haue doon it/ I thanke you as moche as I may/ and
it is wel reason that ye therfore be rewarded/ And yet sayd
Vyenne to Parys/ knowe ye for trouthe/ that it is long sythe
that I haue desyred to knowe/ & yet desyre strongely to knowe 5
it/ wherfore yf ye wyl do me ony playsyr/ I praye you that
ye say to me the trouthe/ wythout leuyng of ony onely thynge
or word/

Thenne sayd parys moche humbly with grete shamefastnes
that he had to vtter the folye that he had enterprysed/ 10
Ryght honourable and fayr lady I am not worthy to be
named hym whiche hath doon thys/ whyche it hath pleased
you to demaunde of me/ but notwythstondyng that I be a
man of lytel estate I humbly supplye you that in caas ye shal
fynde dysplaysyr in my wordes that it playse you to pardonne 15
me/ and that ye take noo dysplaysyr in that I shal say/ for
your noblesse shal not be the lasse in valure/ For my caas
enforceth me to say that/ whyche is to me folye to thynke/
Thenne Parys al shamefast and in grete reuerence knelyng
vpon hys knee sayd/ Ryght worshypful damoysel parys your 20
Indigne seruaunt is he of whome ye haue spoken & demaunded/
& shal to you obeye and serue in al thynges that ye haue me
demaunded/ For sythe that I haue had ony rememberaunce/
my wylle & my thought hath be submysed to your persone
and shal be as longe as I shal lyue/ Thenne sayd vyenne/ Parys 25
my swete frende it is not now tyme that I make ansuer to your
wordes/ for it shold be ouerlonge to recounte/ But that not
wythstondyng I wyl wel that ye knowe that your loue
destrayneth me so strongely/ that there is no thynge in the
world that I loue soo moche as you/ wherfore abyde in good 30
hope Ioyously/ for yf it playse god ye shal see that thys
whyche I say [b v^v] shal be trewe/ Thenne sayd parys/ Madame
who may thynke the Ioyouste in whyche I am by your ansuer
whiche is to me ryght swete/ For I neuer supposed to haue
had so swete an ansuer of you/ but for to haue endured in 35
payne & in languysshyng/ For not onely to me/ but vnto a
kyng shold be ouer moche to haue your loue/ & I praye god

that I may doo suche thynges as may be to you playsaunt/
and that I neuer lyue to do to you thynge that shold desplayse
you/ ne torne you to melancolye/ & thus departed that one
fro that other in gretter loue than tofore/ and took terme to
see eche other ageyn as hastely as they myght/ and vyenne 5
retorned more Ioyously than she shewed/ and wente in to hyr
moders chambre/ and after the bysshop departed/ & parys
accompanyed hym vnto his paleys and took leue of hym/ &
retorned home vnto hys faders lodgyng/ & after tolde to
edward hys felowe/ alle the parlament that he had had wyth 10
vyenne/ & Edward sayd to hym/ fayre brother and frende/
herein is no Iape ne truffes/ but I praye you that ye do your
thynges secretly for there ben many false tonges And Vyenne
was moche more Ioyous than she had ben accustomed/ and
Parys also/ And the sayd Parys & edward hys felowe made 15
grete chyualryes & dyd grete armes/ whyche were moche
playsaunt to the fayre vyenne/ Thenne it happed that after
certeyn tyme seyng the dolphyn that hys doughter was come
to xv yere of age/ treated for to gyue to hyr an husbond/ And
many tymes he had ben requyred of many noble pryncẽs but 20
by cause he had but hyr onely and no moo sones ne doughters/
vnnethe he wold consente And in treatyng thus of maryage
Parys herde somme thynges wherof he was sore ennoyed in
hym self/ and thought/ why thynke not I to haue this noble
lady whyche is so moche desyred of so many noble pryncẽs 25
& barons/ and sore bewaylled hym self/ and dyd soo moche
that he spake to vyenne and sayd/ O swete Vyenne/ where
is your fayr and agreable promesse that ye made to me whan
I departed fro you/ and how may it be/ that your fader speketh
for to marye you/ 30

Whan vyenne herde Parys speke in thys manere/ she sayd
to hym parys yf my fader speke to me of maryage/ it
is noo grete meruaylle/ for I may not deffende hym/
Neuertheles I haue not consented to ony maryage/ And ye
knowe wel that maryage is [b vj^r] nothyng worth/ wythout 35
the consentyng of bothe partyes/ wherfore I praye you to be
contente/ for I promyse to you that I shal neuer haue man in

mariage but you/ and I wold that it shold be shortly accomplysshed yf it pleased god/ honestly & Iustly and not in synne ne in ordure/ Therfore I wyl that ye assaye one thynge/ which shal be moche dyffycyle to doo and ryght peryllous/ but neuertheles it byhoueth that it be doon/ thenne sayd Parys/ 5 honourable lady/ that whyche shal playse you to commaunde me/ I shal accomplisshe it with good hert though I shold deye/ & thenne sayd Vyenne/ I wyl that Incontynent ye say to your fader/ that he goo to my lord my fader/ and requyre hym that he gyue me in maryage to you/ and that herein 10 ther be no deffaute/ & whan Parys herde the wylle & desyre of vyenne/ he was quasi al abasshed & sayd/ Ryght honourable lady & how/ wyl ye that I deye thus/ I praye you yf it playse you/ that it be not doo/ Thenne vyenne sayd sette ye so lytel by me/ that ye wyl not enterpryse this/ Alas where is your 15 entendement/ Certes it must nedes be doon/ Incontynent Parys ansuerd/ worshypfull lady/ sythe it playseth you/ I shal accomplysshe your commandement though I shold deye therfore an hondred thousand tymes & thus took leue of vyenne and wente to hys fader Incontynent and sayd to hym/ Dere 20 fader alwaye ye haue shewed to me grete loue/ wherfore I byseche almyȝty god that he rewarde you lyke as I desyre/ Dere & honourable fader I wold praye you of one thynge/ and by cause it is doubtous I wyl that ye promyse it to me tofore I say it to you/ for ellys I wyl not say it vnto you/ & hys 25 fader sayd to hym/ My sone there is nothyng in the world that I may doo for the/ but I shal accomplysshe it by the grace of god/ therfor say to me thy playsyr & wylle/ & thenne parys tolde to hys fader a parte of the pryuete and promesse that he had wyth vyenne/ by cause he shold wyth the better 30 wylle doo that/ whyche he wold requyre hym/ Thenne sayd parys to his fader/ the prayer that I praye & requyre you is/ that it playse you to say to the dolphyn/ that he gyue to me hys doughter to wyf and in maryage/ And I humbly byseche you that herein ye wyl not faylle me/ & messire Iaques heryng 35 hys sone thus speke/ almoost he was fro hym self for the grete folye þᵗ he sayd to hym/ & he sayd in repreuyng hym that he neuer shold speke more of that fayte/ for he wold not deye

for hys doughter/ and [b vj^v] that he shold demaunde of hym
somme other thynge/ for it were grete folye to speke to hym
of suche a thynge/ And parys sayd worshypful fader/ as moche
peryllous is it to me as to you/ therfor I am not abasshed
thugh ye reffused to doo it/ But loue enforceth and con- 5
streyneth me so strongely/ that I am half confused/ and am
as wel contente that he do it not/ as to doo it/ but that ye
do your deuoyr onely/ and so longe parys prayed hys fader/
that he[1] promysed hym to doo it/

¶ *How messire Iaques demaunded of the doulphyn hys doughter
vyenne in maryage for hys sone Parys/*

Thenne went messire Iaques to the dolphyn all chaunged 10
of colour and sayd to hym/ My ryght redoubted and
souerayn lord a certeyn requeste is made to me/ whyche
I must say vnto you/ the whiche me semeth is of passyng
lytel reason/ and therfore it must be at your mercy/ and in
caas ye fynde therin dysplaysyr/ that ye pardonne me/ and 15
to take noo regarde to my grete folye/ The doulphyn trustyng
in the grete wysedom of messire Iaques graunted hym to say
what someuer he wold/ Thenne sayd messire Iaques/ Myn hye
and souerayn lord/ Parys my sone hath prayed me so moche
that I shold requyre of you vyenne your doughter to be hys 20
wyf/ the whiche thynge is not onely to say/ but also to thynke
grete presumpsyon and grete folye/ but the loue of my sone
constrayneth me soo strongely/ that by force I must say it to
you/ And sodeynly the doulphyn was moeued in grete felonnye/
and wold not suffre hym to ende hys wordes/ but repreued 25
hym moche hardly sayeng/ vylayne & vassal that thou arte/
how kepest thou my worshyp/ by god I shal wel chastyse
you/ that ye shal neuer thynke suche thynges/ and comaunded
hym that Incontynent he shold departe thens/ and that neuer
he ne hys sone shold come in hys syght/ wherfore messire 30
Iaques departed thens moche rebuked holdyng doun hys
heed/ and retorned in to hys hous/ & tolde to hys sone Parys

[1] be C.

[*Paris and Vienne*]

al that had be sayd and doon bytwene hym & the Doulphyn/
wherof Parys thanked moche hys fader/

The doulphyn wente in grete thou3t thurgh the paleys
hauyng grete Indygnacyon and alle angry in soo moche
that none durst speke to hym ne come in his waye/ and
he beyng thus in thys manere [b vij^r] he sente for his doughter
vyenne & made hyr to come to hym/ and sayd to hyr/ we
haue had wordes of grete dysplaysyr/ Thys vyllayne messyre
Iaques hath sayd to vs that we shold gyue you to wyf and in
maryage to hys sone Parys/ Aduyse you what wysedom it
were/ by god or that I shold do it/ I wold rather make you
a nonne or a menchon/ & it shal not be longe to/ but that ye
shal be hyely maryed/ so that ye shal holde you contente/ &
here I swere to you that yf it were not for the grete seruyces
that he hath doon to me Incontynent I shold do smyte of hys
hede/ & whan vyenne sawe hyr fader in so grete angre ayenst
messyre Iaques & hys sone/ she sente for to seche Edward for
to come speke to hyr/ & whan Edward was come Vyenne sayd
to hym/ Edward it is soo that my fader is moche angry ayenst
messire Iaques & ayenst parys wherof I haue grete dysplaysyr
& haue grete doubte that my fader wyl do somme harme to
Parys/ & therfore I wyl that ye say to hym/ that he kepe
hym self in the moost secretest wyse that he may/ and I shal
also see the manere yf I may appease his felonnye and angre/
Thenne edward Incontynent took leue of vyenne/ & went &
sayd to paris all that vyenne had sayd to hym & sayd fayr
brother/ me semeth that it were good that ye departed oute
of this contrey for to absente you for a space of tyme For it
may be that to the doulphyn shal longe endure hys angre/ as
I vnderstonde by that whyche vyenne hath sayd to me/
Thenne ansuerd Parys/ sythe that ye haue counceylled me soo
I shal so do/ not wythstondyng that it shal be to me a sorouful
& an heuy departyng/ but er I departe I shal take leue of
Vyenne though I shold deye/

[*Paris and Vienne*]

Thenne Parys dyd soo moche that he spake vnto vyenne on a derke nyght at a lowe wyndowe/ where as they myght wel say what they wold/ I am certeyn sayd vyenne that my fader hath wylle to hurte you/ wherof I lyue in grete melancolye/ For in al the world is no thynge that I loue so moche as you/ & yf by aduenture ye deye I wyl not lyue/ Thenne sayd parys/ honourable[1] lady it semeth me beste that I departe fro hens a certeyn tyme tyl my lord your fader be more peased & hath passed hys euyll wylle/ how be it/ that it shal be to me a moche sorouful thynge to wythdrawe me fro you/ For my lyf shal be moche heuy/ Neuertheles I shal accomplysshe your wylle in alle that ye shall [b vij^v] commaunde me/ what someuer come therof/ And vyenne seyng the good wylle of parys after many wordes she sayd to hym/ Parys my frende I knowe well the grete loue that ye bere to me/ & sythe it so is/ I swere to you by my fayth/ that ye shal neuer departe fro thys cyte wythoute that I goo wyth you/ For it is my wylle/ wherfore assone as ye may/ make you redy of al thynges necessarye/ and fynde ye the manere that we may escape oute of the royame of fraunce/ and that we may goo in to somme other lordshyppe/ where as we may lyue Ioyously and surely Neuertheles tofore or we departe from hens I wyl that ye promyse two thynges/ The fyrst is/ that ye touche not my body vnto the tyme that we be lawfully maryed/ The second is that ysabeau parte in al the goodes that we shal haue/ and other thynge wyl I not as for thys present tyme/ but that onely our departyng may be shortely/ and I shal pourueye somme Iewels & money for our necessyte/ and al thys Parys promysed to hyr/ and eche departed fro other for tadresse suche thynges as to them shold be necessarye/

Whan Parys was departed fro vyenne he wente to a man named george and sayd to hym/ George my frende alwaye I haue trusted in you/ and haue alwaye loued you/ wherfore I praye you now that to thys that I shal say you ye faylle me not/ for I promyse you ye shal not lese

[1] hanourable C.

[Paris and Vienne]

therby/ and George promysed to hym to doo al that shal be
to hym possyble wyth ryght good hert/ & thenne Parys sayd
to hym/ knowe ye for cartayn that I haue wrath & rancour
to a man of thys toune for certayn desplaysyr that he hath
doon to me/ wherfor I wyl slee hym/ and Incontynent as I
haue slayne hym/ I wyl departe out of the royame of Fraunce/
wherfore I praye you þ^t ye wyl goo to Aygues mortes/ & that
ye there make redy a galeye furnysshed of al thynges necessarye tyl that we be arryued there as we wold be/ And also
I praye you that ye doo ordeyne fro hens to aygues mortes
fro v myle to v myle alwaye good horses redy to thende that
we may surely refresshe vs yf it be nede/ & also I wyl that ye
do thys as secretly as ye may/ and loo here is money ynough
for to furnysshe these sayd thynges/ George sayd/ I shal doo
al thys gladly/ And Incontynent made hym redy/ & whan he
came to aygues mortes he hyred a galeye/ and establisshed al
the passages/ and dyd wel al that parys had charged [b viij^r]
hym/ & came ageyn/ and tolde to parys how he had pourueyed
al that he had charged hym/ wherof parys was moche Ioyous/
& anone parys wente and tolde to Vyenne that alle thynges
that she had comaunded were doon And thenne they concluded that the nexte nyght folowyng that at a certeyn houre
eche of them shold be redy/ thenne he took leue of hyr and
wente home/ and bad George to take two hors out of hys
stable/ and that he shold sadle them and abyde hym wythoute
the cyte in a certayn place tyl he shold come/ & Edward the
felowe of Parys wyste noo thynge of alle thys/ wherof he was
moche abasshed and meruayllously angry whan that he
knewe it/

¶ *How parys ladde awaye vyenne and ysabeau by nyght/*

Whan Parys was pourueyed of money and of al other
thynges beyng to them necessarye/ he wente allone
the secretest wyse þ^t he myȝt and came to the place
emprysed at the houre taken/ and he made a tokene whiche
vyenne knewe And anone vyenne and ysabeau cladde them

36   [*Paris and Vienne*]

in mannes araye & lepen oute of þe castel by a fauce porte/
and so came these two damoyselles to the place where as parys
was allone/ whyche awayted vpon theyr comyng/ & Incontynent they departed and went where as theyr horses were
whom they took & rode as faste as they myght/ and george 5
rode alwaye tofore by cause to knowe wel the waye/ and
whyles they thus rode/ aroos a storme wyth a grete rayne
whyche endured tyl on the morne at nyght/ and thenne they
arryued nygh vnto a lytel towne/ but they entred not by
cause they wold not be knowen/ and wente & lodged them in 10
a lytel chyrche nygh vnto the toun/ where they fonde a
chapelayn whiche receyued them gladly the best wyse he
myght/ & thenne whan the nyght came Parys and the
chapelayn slepte in a lytel hous Ioynyng to the chyrche/
George and parys seruaunte slepten in the stable with the 15
bestes/ And vyenne and ysabeau slepten in the chyrche/ and
in the mornyng erly they wente lyghtly to horsback/ & rode
tyl they came nyghe vnto a ryuer/ whyche was rysen hye by
cause of the rayne that had fallen/ Thenne parys was moche
angry by cause he sawe wel that it was moche peryllous/ & 20
sayd to George/ that he shold serche & aduyse somme good
place where they myght passe ouer/ & george wythdrewe hym
a lytel from them/ and chaas a place whiche [b viij^v] thought
hym good/ and took the ryuer wyth hys hors/ And whan he
was in the myddes of the streme hys hors faylled hym that he 25
was drowned and hys hors also/ ¶Parys seyng that george
was drowned was moche sore abasshed/ and durst make noo
semblaunte/ by cause that fayre vyenne shold haue noo
melancolye/ And after Vyenne demaunded of Parys where
george was bycomen/ and parys answerd to hyr/ that he had 30
sent hym for to serche somme good passage/ and they wold
torne in to the chyrche ageyn tyl George were comen/ And
vyenne ansuerd to hym that it playsed to hyr wel soo to doo/
For she had grete doubte and fere for to passe the water/
¶And whan they were in the chyrche/ Parys was moche 35
aferde to abyde longe in that place/ for he sawe that it
was not sure/ wherfore he demaunded the chapelayn/ yf
they myght in ony wyse passe that water/ And the chapelayn

[Paris and Vienne]

sayd not in thre dayes tyl the water were decreced and aualed/

¶ And parys sayd to hym that he shold goo in to the towne to seche and see yf he myght fynde ony men that wold make a brydge soo that they myȝt passe And that he shold spare for no money/ For I shal paye to them as moche as they wyl haue/ & the chapelayn sayd that he shold doo hys beste/ Thus dyd Parys noo thynge but thynke how they myght passe the ryuer/ Now leue we Parys and torne we to the doulphyn/ whych had lost his fayre doughter vyenne/

¶ *How the doulphyn[1] dyd doo serche and seche vyenne by hys seruauntes/*

On the morne that vyenne was loste & departed fro the hous of hyr fader/ & that the doulphyn knewe it/ he supposed to haue goon oute of hys wytte/ & al the courte was troubled/ & sente hastely men on horsback & a fote by dyuers partyes the moost secretely that he myght/ & prayed them that they shold brynge home to hym vyenne quyck or dede/ It happed by aduenture that one of his men a fote that was sente to seche Vyenne came in to the towne where as the chapelayn was comen to seche men to make the brydge/ The foteman demaunded euery man yf they had seen two damoyselles whyche were fledde fro the doulphyns courte/ Thenne the chapelayn said to hym that it was not longe syth suche tweyne departed wyth other men ¶ And the man supposed that the sayd chapelayn had sayd it [cj^r] in Iape or in mockyng/ And sayd that the Doulphyn was moche angry/ and had sworne that yf ony man or woman knewe where they were and shewed it not/ that he shold make them to lose theyr hedes/ And whan the chapelayn herde these wordes he remembred hym of them that were hyd in hys hous/ And in grete drede sayd to hym/ that he shold tarye there a lytel/ & that for the loue of my lord doulphyn he wold gladly seche for them/ and assone as he myght fynde tydynges of them he shold lete hym wyte/ And so departed fro thens/ and retorned

[1] doulpyn C.

38   [*Paris and Vienne*]

home ageyn/ and tolde al thys to parys/ and what he had
herde in the toune/ sayeng also that he doubted that it was
for them of hys companye/ wherfore he sayd to hym ferther-
more/ syr I praye you that ye departe from hens/ and suffre
not that I lese my lyf/ but take ye the beste counceyl ye   5
can/ For there ben fyfty men on horsback that seche you/
whan Parys herde hym say this it nedeth not to demaunde
yf he were heuy and melancolyous/ and for the grete sorowe
that he had he chaunged al hys colour/ And he sayd to the
chapelayn/ I praye you that ye tarye a lytel & I shal make 10
you an ansuer/ & thenne Parys went to vyenne/ for to telle
to hir al thys feat/ And whan Vyenne sawe hym entre/ and
so chaunged in hys colour sayd to paris/ what tydynges brynge
ye whyche are so pale and your colour chaunged/ I praye you
as hertely as I can that it playse you to telle me/ Thenne 15
Parys sayd to hyr The tydynges that I brynge ben euyl for
you and for me/ For shortly shal be accomplisshed our
aduenture/ and therfore I wyl slee my self/ and also he said
complaynyng/ O god how my lyf is sorowful and heuy to
haue brought thys excellent lady as ye ar in suche daunger/ 20
O good god why gaf thou not to me the deth tofore or that
I fette hir out of hyr faders hous/ O alas my fader and my
moder what shal befalle of you/ whan the doulphyn shal
knowe/ that I haue stolen from hym hys doughter/ ¶O my
good felowe Edward why counceylled not I wyth the tofore 25
or I had doon thys folye And after he retorned to vyenne
sayeng/ and what shal falle of you my lady/ whan your fader
shal see you/ Certes I thynke that how cruel that he be/ whan
he shal see your noble persone/ his hert shal not suffre to do
you ony harme/ O god almyghty do to me that grace þ^t I onely 30
may bere the payn of this fayt & none other/ O lady vnhappy
was that day for you and for me whan [cj^v] fyrst ye had
acqueyntaunce of me/ And whan Parys had fynysshed hys
complaynte/ he tolde to Vyenne al that the chapelayn had
sayd to hym/ And forthwyth as a persone despayred/ took   35
hys swerde and wold haue ryuen it thurgh hys body/ And
Vyenne as vertuouse and valyaunte took to hyr hert/ and
took the swerde fro hym and comforted hym and sayd/ ¶O

[Paris and Vienne]

free knyght/ my Ioye/ my lyf/ and my solace/ what wyl ye
doo/ knowe ye not wel/ that who that sleeth hym self wytyngly/
sleeth the soule and the body/ and yf ye deye/ I assure you
I shal deye also/ and so shal ye be cause of my deth as wel as
of your owne O Parys where is your wysedom and your 5
prowesse/ Now whan ye shold haue moste strengthe & moost
vertuous courage ye be aferde/ O my knyght thys is noo newe
thynge that the persones that lyuen in thys world haue
trybulacyons/ of what someuer lygnage they be/ Certes thys
is not the courage of one so valyaunte knyght as ye be/ For 10
now whome that ye ought to comforte/ she must now comforte
you/ And therfor my fayr brother and frende I praye you as
moche as ye may/ that Incontynente ye departe fro hens/ and
that ye goo your waye/ and yf ye do not so I shal slee my self
wyth your swerde/ For your departyng is as greuous to me/ as 15
myn shal be to you/ but it byhoueth to eschewe of two euyls
the werse/ And also ye ought to consydere one thyng/ that
not wythstondyng the grete faulte and trespaas that I haue
made to my fader/ yet therfore he shal not put me to deth/
consydered the grete loue that he hath alway had toward 20
me/ and yf ye were taken/ I wote wel that ye and I shold
bothe deye/ And yet I haue good hope/ that myn entencyon
shal come vnto a good ende/ For be ye sure though he neuer
pardonne me/ I shal neuer haue other husbond but you and
that I promyse you by my fayth/ But alle waye of one thyng 25
I praye you/ that for none other lady ye forgete not me/ And
whan ye shal be in another contreye wryte vnto me of your
aduenture/ And to thende that ye the better remembre me
loo here is a rynge of gold wyth a dyamonde/ the which I
praye you that ye wyl kepe for the loue of me 30

¶ *How Parys departed from Vyenne/ and lefte hyr in the chyrche/*

After moche other langage paris kyssed vyenne wyth grete
syghes and [c ij^r] thoughtes/ and she comforted hym the
best wyse she myght/ in prayeng our lord Ihesu Cryste
that in short tyme she myght see hym/ lyke as hyr herte

desyred moost of ony thynge that was in the world/ And
thenne Parys departed fro Vyenne wyth grete sorowe and
heuynesse/ And took his waye wyth hys seruaunte tyl he
came to the ryuer where they coude not tofore haue passed/
and as despayred doubted noo thynge but entred therin/ and 5
the water was soo aualed that they passed wythoute ony peryl/
And they rode two dayes wythoute ony mete/ for they durst
not passe thurgh ony toun/ And they passed tyl they came
to aygues mortes/ And there he founde the galeye that george
had hyred/ whyche anone he took/ and so longe saylled and 10
rowed tyl that they arryued at Gene/ Parys made meruayllous
countenaunces in the galeye/ that alle they that were therin/
had supposed he had be a fool/ for allewaye he was pensyf/ and
ymagynatyf/ and vnnethe wold speke ne say a word/ ¶ Thenne
whan he was at gene he hyred hym a lodgyng & lyued there 15
in grete heuynesse & sorowe/ Now leue we to speke of Parys
and retorne we to vyenne whyche abode in the chapelayns
hous

¶ *How vyenne was founde in the chyrche by a foteman/ and how
she was brought ageyn to hyr fader/*

Whan Parys was departed fro vyenne she abode allone
wyth ysabeau makyng the grettest sorowe of the 20
world that it was a grete pyte to byholde/ lyke as she
had as leef to deye as to lyue/ And whan she was wel wery of
wepyng/ and that it was force that she must retorne to the
mercy of hyr fader the doulphyn/ she appeased hyr self/ And
anone the chapelayn went for to seche the foteman and 25
brought hym in to the chyrche/ And whan Vyenne sawe hym/
she knewe hym wel/ For she had oftymes seen hym in hyr
faders hows/ And thys man sayd to hyr alle hys charge/ & that
many knyghtes were oute for to seche hyr/ And Vyenne sayd
to hym goo & telle them that thou hast founden me here/ & 30
brynge them hyther/ Thenne the man wente & fonde the
knyghtes that thenne were comen in to the towne/ and tolde
to them how he had founden hyr/ & that they shold come
with hym & he wold brynge them to the place where she was/

whan þe kny3tes herde these tydynges anon eche made grete
haste tyl they cam to hyr/ thenne whan they were [cij^v] tofore
vyenne they salewed hyr and sayd to hyr that the doulphyn
had doo seche hyr in dyuers contreyes/ and after they comforted hyr/ and sayd that she shold not be aferde of hyr fader/ 5
for he wold doo to hyr no desplaysyr/ for he[1] shal haue so
grete Ioye/ whan he shall see you/ that he shal pardonne you
and appease hys yre/

¶ And than Incontynent they wente to horsbacke/ and
brought forth the chapelayn wyth hyr to thende that he shold 10
excuse hyr tofore hyr fader/ and tolde how she was pure and
clene of hyr body/

Now sayth thystory that whan Vyenne was comen tofore
hyr fader the doulphyn/ he made toward hyr heuy and
euyll chere/ But not wythstondyng Vyenne kneled doun 15
on bothe hyr knees to the erthe sayeng and in wepyng/ Redoubted fader I see wel and knowe in my self that I haue
mesprysed and faylled toward you/ wherof I haue grete
desplaysyr/ Neuertheles folysshe loue hath enforced me to
loue hym/ whyche is wel worthy to be byloued of the moost 20
grettest lady of the Royame of fraunce allewaye seen the
noblenes that is in hym/ For I wene that in alle the world is
none to hym lyke ne pareylle/

¶ And also I thynke that I am not the first that haue
trespaced by semblable reasons/ wherfore redoubted fader I 25
am in your mercy/ and take of me vengeaunce/ suche as shal
playse you/ and to me chastysement/ and example to other
Neuertheles I wyl wel that ye knowe and that I swere by my
soule/ that I am as pure and clene of my body as I was that
day that I departed fro hens/ And loo here is the chapelayn 30
whyche can say to you the trouthe/ And thenne the chapelayn
tolde how she came wyth iij men of whom that one was a
moche fayre knyght yonge & curtoys the whyche I byleue is
drowned in passyng a ryuer/ And they were in myn hous/ and
the two damoyselles slept to gyder in the chyrche/ and the 35
knyght slepte wyth me/ And the other two slepte in the stable

[1] be C.

42   [*Paris and Vienne*]

with the horses/ Thenne whan the doulphyn herde these
tydynges he had ry3t grete playsyr/ of which he made noo
semblaunte/ and gaf to the chapelayn moche money & grete
yeftes/ and bad hym retorne/ ¶After the doulphyn took
vyenne by the hande/ in repreuyng hyr moche gretely/ and   5
lad hyr in to hyr moders chambre wyth ysabeau/ for hir moder
was seke of the grete sorowe that she had for hyr doughter/ and
there the [ciij^r] moder blamed them bothe two/ And ysabeau
sayd that vyenne was as pure and clene of hyr body as she
was the day that she departed/ Alas sayd the doulphyn/ thou 10
hast put vs in the moost grettest shame of þ^e world And I
promyse that alle they that haue consented therto shal be wel
punysshed/ and in especyal that euyl traytre Parys whych is
cause of al thys fayte and yf euer I may haue hym I shal make
dogges deuoure hym and also bothe ye tweyne shal suffre   15
therfore grete penytence/ Thenne sayd vyenne wepyng/ I see
wel and knowe that ye haue entencion to do to me moche gryef
and harm/ and I see wel that my lyf shal not longe endure/
Therfore I swere to you in good fayth/ that there is noo man
in the world that I so moche loue as I doo hym whom ye   20
so menace and thretene/ For in hym I haue my thought &
courage wythoute euer to faylle hym/ and yf ye shortly gyue
to me my penaunce/ so moche shortly shal be my deth/ And
yf ye suffre me to endure it longe/ so moche more shal I bere
it/ and my soule shal be the more sure tofore almyghty god/ & 25
knowe ye for certayn that for hym and hys loue I am redy to
deye/

    Thenne the doulphyn yssued out of the chambre in grete
Indygnacyon and commaunded that the fader of Parys shold
be put in an euyl pryson/ And that al hys goodes shold be   30
taken fro hym/ And also that vyenne & ysabeau shold be
enclosed in a chambre/ and that wel lytell mete shold be gyuen
to them/ and moche he menaced and thretened them/ and
thus they abode a longe tyme in that chambre/ and contynuelly
Vyenne dremed of Parys/   35

    ¶And whan she myght haue ony space to speke to Edward
felowe of Parys/ she requyred hym that he shold serche yf he
myght haue ony tydynges of parys/ and that he shold lete hyr

[Paris and Vienne] 43

knowe therof/ ¶In thys maner vyenne passed hyr tyme in
grete sorowe & in grete thought alle waye desyryng for to here
somme tydynges of that noble knyght Parys/

When Vyenne had ben a grete tyme in thys manere/ The
doulphyn bythought hym that thenne hys doughter
Vyenne had been wel chastysed/
¶And thenne the Doulphyn fader of Vyenne ordeyned that
she came oute of pryson/ And thenne he purposed to gyue to
hyr an husbond/ and sette hyr in hyr fyrst estate/ wherof alle
the [ciij^v] courte was moche Ioyous/ and in especyal Edward
felowe of Parys/ ¶And after certayn tyme the doulphyn
wrote to the Erle of Flaunders that he wold doo marye hys
doughter vyenne wherupon he requyred hym that he wold
gyue to hym counceyll in thys mater/ For it was vnto hym
chargeable/ And duryng the tyme that vyenne was oute of
pryson hyr herte was neuer in reste/ but euer she was heuy
and sorouful for hyr swete and faythful frende parys/ whome
she myght not see/ and knewe not whether he were dede or
a lyue/ And whan the doulphyn sawe hyr so heuy/ On a day
he sayd to hyr/ My swete doughter/ wherfore be ye so soroyful/
gyue your self to playsyr/ For as to me I remembre nomore
the thynges passed/ And there is noo thynge in the world that
ye demaunde me but I shal doo it for you/ And thenne vyenne
whyche had not forgeten Parys sayd to hym/ Honourable
fader yf I were sure of the thynges passed that they were
forgoten by you/ I shold be more sure than I am/ but I byleue
fermely/ that ye haue them yet in your remembraunce/ For
ye holde alwaye messyre Iaques in pryson the fader of Parys/
whyche is not culpable of ony parte of thys dede ne cause/ And
yf ye wold do to me soo moche grace that ye wold pardonne
hym and rendre to hym al hys goodes & thynges I shold be
moche Ioyous/ And the doulphyn for the playsyr of hys
doughter sayd to hyr/ that it wel playsed to hym/ and Incon-
tynent¹ the doulphyn dyd do delyuer messyre Iaques out of
pryson/ and dyd do retorne to hym al hys goodes and thynges
that had be taken from hym/ wherof messyre Iaques had grete

¹ Incontynt C.

playsyr/ for yf he had abyden lenger in pryson he had be dede
for hungre/ for there was none that comforted hym but
edward/ whiche comforted hym the best wyse he myght/ &
gaf to hym dayly that whyche was necessarye for hys lyf/
whan vyenne knewe that messyre Iaques was oute of pryson/ 5
she was moche Ioyeful and had grete playsyr/ Neuertheles al
the consolacyon of vyenne was whan she myght speke wyth
edward of hyr loue Parys/ And thus she passed hyr tyme in
ryght grete payne and heuynesse the beste wyse she myght/

When the Erle of flaunders had redde the letters of the 10
doulphyn & vnderstood that he wold marye his
doughter vyenne whych was [ciiij^r] of the age of xv
yere/ he trayted that she shold haue of two barons that one/
that is to wete the sone of the kyng of englond/ or the sone of
the duke of bourgoyne/ whyche thenne had grete renommee 15
in fraunce/ and that was for the grete prowesse that was in
hym/ and the sayd erle made thys sayd traytye/ & sente word
vnto the doulphyn/ that hym semed best that the sone of the
duc of bourgoyn were beste for hyr/ by cause that it shold be
grete playsyr to the Kynge of fraunce/ and that he was a noble 20
knyght and of grete prowesse/ and whan the doulphyn had
receyued these letters fro therle of Flaunders/ he sente to the
kyng of fraunce to wyte of hym whyche shold best playse hym
of these two prynces aforesayd that shold haue his doughter/
For whome that he wold shold haue hyr/ wherof þ^e kyng had 25
grete playsyr/ and reputed it to hym grete honour/ And he
sente to hym worde/ that it shold playse hym best that he
maryed wyth the sone of the duc of bourgoyn hys neuew/ and
in so doyng he shold doo to hym ryght grete playsyr/ and wold
do as moche for hym whan tyme and place requyreth/ And 30
seyng the doulphyn the wylle of the kyng of fraunce sente
worde to therle of flaunders/ that he had counseylled wyth hys
barons & also that it was the wylle of the kyng of fraunce that
his doughter shold be maryed to the sone of the duc of
bourgoyne/ And thenne therle laboured so moche in thys 35
mater that he made the sayd sone of the duc to agree as for
hys partye/

[Paris and Vienne] 45

¶ *How Parys sente a letter to hys felowe Edward/*

Now late vs leue to speke of thys mater/ and retorne we vnto Parys whyche abode in the cyte of gene moche heuy/ and whyles thys maryage was in trayty Parys dwelled in gene oute of al Ioyes and playsaunses worldly/ & al for the loue that he had to the fayr vyenne whome he 5 had soo moche at his hert/ And abode alwaye in hys lodgyng allone/ and bycame so deuoute and soo humble toward god/ that it was grete meruaylle/ and also for the good countenaunces that he made/ he was moche wel byloued of al the peple of the cyte and they helde hym for a noble man/ and 10 sayd he must nedes be the sone of a grete lord/ And Parys beyng in thys manere had grete desyre to haue tydynges of vyenne/ and what was hyr aduenture/ And anone ordeyned two letters/ that one to [c iiij^v] hys fader/ & that other to hys felawe Edward/ Of whyche the letter to hys fader sayd in thys 15 manere/

Ryght dere & honourable syr and fader playse it you to wete that I am moche sorouful and heuy of my cruel aduenture/ and also I endure grete heuynes/ sorowe and afflyctyon/ doubtyng that for me ye haue suffred grete payne 20 and trybulacyon/ and I late you wete that I am at genes/ & dwelle in a lodgyng allone deposed fro al Ioyes and consolacyons mondayne/ For myn entendement is to serue god and our lady fro hens forth/ & purpose that ye shal see me nomore/ for I wyl departe & goo thurgh the world to seche holy 25 pylgrymages/ And yf by aduenture I shal deye tofore that ye shal see me/ I praye you that it may playse you that I deye not in your euyl wylle/ but humbly[1] byseche you that it playse you to pardonne me/ and to gyue to me your benedyctyon/ Also dere syr and fader I pray you & supplye that my dere 30 brother and felowe Edward ye wyl take in my name and place/ and that he be recommaunded as your sone in stede of me/ as wel in your herytage as in other thynges/ and the grace of the holy ghoost be wyth you/ Recomaunde me to my moder &c/ And the letter of Edward sayd thus/ 35

[1] humby C.

[Paris and Vienne]

Dere and specyal brother and synguler frende edward the peryl of paris and of hys aduenture is poursyewed of alle euyl and cruel fortune/ I comaunde me to you as moche as I may say or thynk Neuertheles lyke as we haue ben accustomed to wryte letters of loue and of chyualrye/ 5 Now I must wryte letters anguysshous of sorowe and of euyl fortune/ for alas I am vnhappy al allone in a strange contre/ & exyled fro al Ioyes and fro alle playsyr/ and out of al worldly playsaunce thynkyng nyght & day on the bele vyenne/ the whyche I thynke that for me hath suffred mortal sorowe/ and 10 I say to you that yf I knewe that for me she suffred payne and sorowe I shold be in despayr/ for I am worthy for to be punysshed cruelly for that fayte & none other wherfore I praye god and alle hys sayntes that she may be kepte from al euyl/ and gyue hyr grace to prospere in al good and honour lyke as 15 she is worthy and myn herte desyreth/

¶ My dere broder & felowe the moost dere thynges that I loue in thys world is fyrst the fayr and swete vyenne/ & next you to whom I praye you yf it may [c v^r] be in ony wyse that ye wyl say to hyr in my name/ how that I am lyuyng in genes/ 20 Passyng my lyf moche heuy and sorouful for thabsence of hyr noble persone/ and for the cruel & euyl fortune that hath poursyewed me/ and also say ye to hyr that I crye hyr mercy/ & that it may playse hyr to pardonne me/ yf by me she haue ony dysplaysyr and god knoweth myn entencyon/ & in what 25 trybulacion I lyue And syth that it hath not playsed to our lord/ that we accomplysshe not our desyre & wylle/ we ought to bere it pacyently/ And also ye shal say to hyr/ that I praye and supplye her as moche as I may that she yet take no husbond/ vnto the tyme that she shal see thende of our 30 aduenture/ & after thys I praye you dere broder of the consolacyon of my fader & my moder/ and that ye be to them as a sone/ For seyng the loue that alwaye we haue had to gyder/ I haue wryton to my fader/ that in the stede of me he take you for hys sone/ and that after hys lyf/ he wyl leue to 35 you hys herytage/ for so moche broder & felowe I praye & byseche you that ye be to theym humble and obeyssaunt/ & the better parte shal be youres/ and yf by aduenture ye wryte

[Paris and Vienne]

to me ony letter late the letter be kepte in my faders house/ þe
holy ghoost haue you in hys kepyng/ And he delyuerd thys
letter to a courrour whyche wythin fewe dayes was at vyenne/
and secretely delyuerd hys letters to edward the good knyght/
whan Edward had receyued these letters and knewe that paris
was a lyue/ he had ryght as grete Ioye as ony man coude
thynke or byleue/ Neuertheles he helde þe courrour secretely
in his hous to thende that the dolphyn shold not knowe
therof/ and whan he had herde the letters/ he went to the hous
of messyre Iaques the fader of the noble parys & sayd to
hym/ ¶Messyre Iaques I brynge to you thys letter/ And whan
messyre Iaques had redde the letter/ he coude not be sacyat
of redyng/ he took so grete playsyr therin/ ¶After that he had
redde it at his playsyr/ he prayed Edward to wryte to hym
an ansuer wel at large of alle that was byfallen syth hys
departyng/ & thys doon edward departed fro hym/ & wente
vnto beale vyenne/ whome he fonde moche heuy and sorouful
for hir loue and frende parys/ and Edward sayd/ honourable
lady/ & how is it/ that ye be thus heuy/ and vyenne sayd to
hym/ alas fayr broder Edward/ I haue good reason and cause
to be heuy For myn herte abydeth thynkyng day & nyght on
my good [c v^v] knyght Parys/ and I knowe not whether he be
alyue or dede/ of whyche thynge I moche desyre to knowe/
For yf he be deed I am cause therof/ And certes yf he be dede
I may not lyue after hym/ yf our lord wold doo soo moche
grace that he be a lyue/ fayn wold I knowe in what londe he
is/ to thende that I my3t sende to hym a lytel money/ soo that
he haue noo necessyte for hys persone/ And edward sayd to
hyr/ Madame what wyll ye gyue me/ yf I telle to[1] you good
tydynges and sure of hym/

¶Thenne sayd Vyenne/ by my fayth there is noo thyng that
I haue in thys world/ whyche I may gyue wyth myn honour/
but that I shal gyue it to you Thenne sayd Edward/ loo here
is a letter whyche he hath sente to me/ and whan vyenne sawe
the letter she opened it and redde it al allonge/ & whan she
had redde it she had soo grete Ioye/ that hyr semed god had
appyered to hyr/ and the Ioye that she had in hyr hert shewed

[1] te C.

wel in hyr vysage/ For sythe that she departed fro parys she
had not so good vysage ne chere as she had thenne & whan
the solace had ynough endured Edward sayd to hyr Madame
gyue to me ageyn my letter/ that I may make to hym an
ansuer/ And Vyenne sayd it pleseth me moche that ye make 5
to Parys my swete frende an ansuer/ but surely the letter
shal remayne wyth me/ Thenne he sayd/ Madame haue ye
not promysed to gyue to me that thyng that I shal demaunde
you/ yes sayd she/ Thenne edward sayd I desyre ne wyll haue
none other thynge/ but that ye gyue to me my letter/ for 10
assone shal I gyue to you my lyf/ but and yf ye wyl demaunde
ony other thynge/ I wyl wel/ Thenne sayd Edward I am
contente that the letter abyde wyth you/ & after he ordeyned
another letter to Parys which sayd in this manere/

¶ *How Edward sente ansuer of his letter to Parys/ whyche abode
in the cyte of genes/*

Ryght dere brother frende and felowe parys/ your fader 15
and your moder grete you wel/ the whiche haue suffred
for you moche dysease/ payne and desplaysyr/ and in
especyal your fader whiche hath longe been in pryson/ & alle
hys goodes were taken fro hym/ and also I certefye you that
by the grace of god and at the request and prayer of Vyenne/ 20
the doulphyn hath pardonned hym alle hys euyl wylle/ and
delyuerd hym oute of pryson & restored to hym alle hys goodes
ageyn/ And plese it you to wete fayre [c vj^r] brother that
vyenne hath had so moche Ioye and so grete playsyr whan
she had knowleche that ye were a lyue/ that it is wonder to 25
byleue/ For al hyr consolacyon was for to haue tydynges of
you/ & she recommaundeth hyr to you as moche as she may/
& hath moche grete desyre to see you & also prayeth you not
to wythdrawe you fro hyr ne fro that contreye/ but that ye
wryte ofte to hyr of your estate/ And she sendeth to you an 30
eschaunge of thre thousand floryns/ of whiche she wyl that ye
take your playsyr & Ioye/ for al hyr hope is in you/ Also ye
shal vnderstonde that she hath be kepte in pryson a certayn

tyme/ but thanked be god she is now oute/ Also I haue shewed
to hyr your letter/ whyche she reteyneth/ and after that she
had redde it/ I myght neuer haue it ageyn/ but she sayd/ that
she had leuer to lese al that she had/ than the said letter & ye
shal knowe that the doulphyn treateth a maryage for hyr the 5
which is the sone of the duc of bourgoyn/ & he hopeth fro day
to day/ that it shal be accomplysshed/ Neuertheles I truste
soo moche in vyenne/ seyng þt whiche she hath sayd to me/
that she wyl neuer haue other husbond but you/ wherfore
lyue ye forth Ioyously in hope/ Dere brother I thanke you as 10
I can or may for the presentacyon that ye haue doon for
me/ your soule be wyth god/ to whome I praye that he kepe
you in hys holy warde & protectyon &c/ whan thys letter was
wryten he delyuerd it to the courrour/ whyche made hasty
Iourneyes so that he arryued at genes/ where as the good 15
knyȝt Parys dwelled and abode/

Whan the noble paris had redde the letter/ & knewe that
vyenne had been in pryson/ almoost for sorowe he was
oute of his wytte cursyng his euyl fortune/ & after he
cursed the day that he was borne & moche dyscomforted hym 20
self/ & also he cursed the doulphyn sayeng/ O cruel fader and
vnconnyng/ how may your hert suffre to put in pryson hyr
that is soo noble a creature/ whyche is ful of al vertues/ that
is the fayre vyenne/ whyche is noo thynge cause of thys fayte/
For I my self onely haue doon it/ & ought to bere allone the 25
penaunce/ alas & wherfore dyd not god to me so moche grace/
that I had be taken in stede of hyr/ O fayre vyenne what
haue I doo for you/ whyche haue suffred soo moche payne for
me/ Thus he made a grete whyle hys sorowe in wepyng
strongely/ After Parys sawe that the fayr vyenne was [cvj^v] 30
retorned in to hyr fyrst estate/ wherof he was moche Ioyous/
& whan he had receyued the eschaunge that vyenne had sente
hym he hyred a moche fayr hous & cladde hym honestly &
rychely & took acqueyntaunce & amytye wyth the grettest
& beste of the cyte/ in so moche they dyd hym moche good 35
and honour/ & thus duellyd parys a grete whyle/ alway
remembryng in hys hert the loue of vyenne/ for alleway hys

[*Paris and Vienne*]

loue encreaced/ And euery moneth they wrote letters eche to other/ of whyche here is made noo mencyon/ for it shold be ouer longe to reherce/ & torne we here in to flaunders for the fayte of the maryage of the excellent vyenne/

Now sayth thystorye that whan therle of Flaunders had accorded the maryage with the duc of bourgoyn he made redy hys sone and apparaylled hym of companye and of horses/ and lete it be knowen to the doulphyn/ that he shold make redy al thynge necessarye/ & that he shold hastely sende to hym his sone/ whan the doulphyn herde these tydynges/ that he/ whome he so moche desyred shold come he was moche Ioyous/ and Incontynent dyd doo make redy many grete & meruayllous festes/ & duryng the same dyd doo make redy hys sone the duc of bourgoyne/ horses and peple for to accompanye hym whiche was a fayre thynge to see/ ¶ And after sent hym to therle of flaunders/ whyche receyued hym wyth grete Ioye & wyth grete honour & fested hym two dayes/ and delyuerd to hym hys sone in his companye/ and sente hym to the doulphyn/ & whan the doulphyn knewe theyr comyng/ he dyd do make redy to receyue hym/ and whan they were by a day Iourneye nygh vnto vyenne/ he rode oute wyth moche grete chyualrye/ & receyued them with moche grete Ioye and playsyr/ & eche made grete feste to other whyche were ouer longe to recounte/ Neuertheles tofore that the doulphyn came to the sone of the[1] duc of bourgoyn/ hee & hys wyf entred in to the chambre of vyenne to whome the doulphyn sayd/ Fayr doughter it was the playsyr of god that I & your moder were to gyder vij yere wythoute hauyng ony chylde/ and in the viij yere our lord comforted vs wyth you/ in whom we haue al our affectyon/ For we haue neyther sone ne doughter but onely you/ ne suppose neuer to haue/ so we truste that by you we haue one/ It is trewe that[2] so as god wyl and hath ordeyned we wyl assemble you to a moche honourable[3] maryage/ the whiche to vs [c vij^r] playseth moche/ for I ensure you the doughter of the Kynge of Fraunce hath moche desyred to haue hym/ that ye shal haue/ for god

[1] she C. [2] thot C. [3] honouble C.

hath endowed hym with so moche good & honour as hert of
knyght may haue/ thus to the playsyr of god/ & of the
vyrgyn marye/ we haue made the maryage of the sone of the
duke of bourgoyne & of you/ wherfor we praye you/ that
therto ye wyl gyue your good wylle & playsyr/ and also that 5
ye wyl haue the maryage agreable/ Thenne vyenne ansuerd
to hyr fader/ Honourable fader & lord I wote wel that thys
that ye entende is for my wele & prouffyt/ But not wythstondyng that I be in age for to marye/ & that in thys maryage
I shold receyue honour more than I am worthy/ Neuertheles 10
I shal not yet be maryed for yf we haue not thys man/ yf it
playse god we shal haue another as good or better/ And
thynke ye not myn honourable lord/ that I say thys for ony
excusacyon/ but it is sythen xv dayes that I haue be euyl dysposed of my persone/ & the maladye that I haue causeth me to 15
take noo playsyr for to be maryed/ For I haue auowed vnto god
neuer to be maryed to thys man ne to none other/ as longe as
I shal be in thys maladye/ ¶Thenne thought the dolphyn that
vyenne sayd it for shamefastnes/ Neuertheles he trauaylled
hyr euery day wyth fayre wordes that she shold consente to 20
thys maryage/ but it auaylled nothyng all that he dyd/ for the
wylle of hir was more in parys than in ony man of the world/

Thenne on the morne the sone of the duc of bourgoyne/ &
the sone of the erle of Flaunders entred in to the cyte of
vyenne/ wherof the doulphyn had grete Ioye & playsyr/ 25
and thys feste endured wel fyftene dayes/ that they dyd no
thynge/ but daunce/ synge/ and dyd other dyuers playsyrs/
and duryng thys feste the doulphyn sayd to the sone of the
duke of bourgoyn to thende that he shold thynke none euyl
by cause he abode so longe or he myght espouse hys doughter/ 30
¶Fayr sone I praye you & byseche that ye take you to playsyr
and Ioye/ And gryeue you noo thynge of thys longe abydyng
here/ for certayn my doughter is so seke/ that vnnethe she
may speke/ whyche doth to hyr grete desplaysyr and shame/
for fayn she wold be out of hyr chambre/ And thenne the sone 35
of the duc of bourgoyn as he that[1] mente but good fayth/

[1] shat C.

byleued it lyghtly/ Neuertheles the doulphyn dyd nothyng
nyȝt [cvij^v] ne day/ but admonested hys doughter one tyme
in fayr wordes/ and another tyme in menaces/ but in no wyse
he coude make hys doughter to consente/ And comaunded
that she shold nothyng haue but brede & water and vyenne 5
abode one day soo in thys manere/ and al thys dyd the
doulphyn/ to thende that she shold consente to the maryage/
and alwaye he dyd to hyr more harme & payne/ & vyenne
was alwaye more harde/ and ferther fro hys desyre/ wherof
the doulphyn had moche grete dysplaysyr/ and not wythoute 10
cause/ & seyng the Doulphyn that hys doughter was soo
Indurate/ he thought that by somme good moyen he wold
sende home ageyn the sone of the duc of bourgoyn for he
doubted that yf he abode longe/ that this feat myght be
dyscouerd/ and he gaf to hym fayr Iewellys/ and after sayd 15
to hym/ Fayre sone I wyl that ye take noo desplaysyr in that
I shal say to you/ Me semeth wel that at thys tyme this
maryage may not goo forth of you and of my doughter/ for
after that I see/ & as me semethe the wylle of god is ferther
than I wold at thys tyme/ For he wyl not that the maryage 20
of you and of my doughter take now effecte/ wherfore I haue
ryght grete desplaysyr in my hert onely for the loue of you/
Thenne the sone of the duc of bourgoyne seyng that at that
tyme he myght doo noo thyng/ toke leue of the Doulphyn and
retorned in to his contree by cause that Vyenne was not in 25
helthe/ and promysed that assone as he myght knowe that she
shold be hool/ he wold retorne for to accomplysshe the mariage
lyke as the doulphyn had promysed to hym/

¶ *How the doulphyn dyd doo enprysonne vyenne by cause that she*
   wold not consente to the maryage to the sone of the duke of
   bourgoyne/

After certayn dayes that the sone of the Duke of bourgoyn
was departed fro the cyte of vyenne/ the doulphyn for 30
grete desplaysyr that he had dyd do come tofore hym
the mayster Iayler of hys pryson/ and dyd doo make wythin

[*Paris and Vienne*]

hys paleys a lytel pryson derke and obscure/ and he dyd do
put vyenne and ysabeau in to that pryson/ and commaunded
that they shold haue nothyng to ete but brede and water/ and
one damoysel in whome the dolphyn trusted shold brynge it
to them And in thys manere vyenne & ysabeau passyd theyr
tyme in grete sorowe/ And thynke not that for thys pryson/
the hert of [c viij^r] vyenne wold in ony wyse consente to the
wylle of hyr fader/ but alway encreaced wyth hyr þe wylle
toward hir swete frende Parys/ and wyth swete wordes she
comforted ysabeau sayeng/ My dere suster abasshe you not
for thys derkenes/ for I haue confydence in god/ that ye shal
haue yet moche welthe/ For my fayr suster/ It is a moche
ryghtful thyng that for the good kny3t parys whyche for me
suffreth so moche payne/ that I suffre thys for hym/ and also
I say to you that al the paynes of this world be nothyng
greuous to me whan I thynke on hys swete vysage/ And in
thys manere that one comforted that other/ in spekyng alle
day of the valyaunte knyght Parys/

¶ *How the sone of the duc of bourgoyn departed fro hys contreye
for to come see the fayre lady Vyenne/*

Whan the sone of the duc of bourgoyne had abyden longe
tyme in hys contree/ On a day he had grete thought of
vyenne/ & that was for the grete beaute of hyr/ and it
dysplesed hym moche that at hys beyng there he had not seen
hyr/ and so concluded to goo & see hyr/ and it was not longe
after that he cam to the dolphyn and the doulphyn receyued
hym moche gladly and with grete honour/ Thenne prayed he
the dolphyn that it myght plese hym to shewe to hym vyenne
also seke as she was/ For in the world was nothyng that he
soo moche desyred to see as hyr/ And the doulphyn seyng the
wylle & desyre of hym wold noo lenger hyde hys courage/ but
sayd to hym/ My fayr sone by the fayth that I owe to god/ I
haue had grete desyre that thys maryage shold be made/ but
my doughter for thys present tyme wyl take noo husbond ne
be maryed/ wherfore I haue grete desplaysyr and that for the

loue of you/ & to thende that ye knowe/ that it holdeth not
on me/ I swere to you that sythe ye departed fro thys toun/
I haue doon hyr to be kepte in a pryson derke and obscure/ and
hath eten nothyng but brede and water onely/ and haue sworn
that she shal not goo oute of pryson tyl she shal consente to 5
haue you in maryage/ And thus I praye you that ye take noo
desplaysyr/ yf at thys tyme ye see hyr not/ for ye may not
faylle to haue grete maryage/ in caas that this faylle you and
thenne he ansuerd/ honourable syr I praye you moche hertely/
syth that it is so/ that er I retorne I may speke to hyr/ and 10
I shal praye hyr as moche as I [c viij^v] shal mowe/ and shal
see yf by ony manere I may conuerte hyr fro hyr wylle/ thenne
sayd the doulphyn he was contente/

Thenne he sente to his doughter clothyng and vestymentes
for to clothe hyr/ and also mete for to ete/ For in two monethes 15
she had eten but brede and water/ wherof she was moche
feble/ and that shewed wel in her vysage/ & thus he dyd by
cause she shold consente to the maryage/ And thenne it was
concluded/ that the sone of the duc of bourgoyn shold come
see hyr and speke with hyr/ and thenne whan Vyenne sawe 20
thys and had receyued all & knewe that the sone of the duc
of bourgoyn shuld come & speke wyth hyr she said to ysabeau
hir damoysel/ fayr suster beholde how my fader & moder wene
by these vestymentes & thys henne that I shold ete to deceyue
me and put me fro my purpoos/ but god forbede that I shold 25
do so/ & thenne she took the henne/ & sayd to hyr that
brought it/ syth it playseth to the sone of the duke to come
& speke to me/ say ye to hym that he may not come these
iij dayes/ & whan he cometh that he brynge with hym the
bysshop of Saynt laurens/ She that had brought to hyr the 30
henne sayd all thys vnto the doulphyn and to dame dyane hir
moder/ ¶Thenne vyenne took the two quarters of the henne
and put them vnder hyr arme hooles/ and helde them there
so longe/ that they stonken moche strongely/ ¶And whan it
came to the thyrd day/ the bysshop of Saynt Laurence and 35
the sone of the Duke of Bourgoyne camen for to see vyenne/
and or they entred they opened a treylle whyche gaf lyght in
to the pryson/

[Paris and Vienne]

¶Thenne whan the sone of the duc sawe Vyenne in the pryson he sayd to hir by grete pyte that he had/ Noble vyenne how wyl ye deye thus for hungre soo folyly by your owne defaulte/ ¶And knowe ye not wel that your fader hath gyuen you to me to haue to my wyf/ wherfore I lyue in grete payne/ and in moche grete sorowe for the duresse of your courage/ wherof ye doo ryght grete synne/ And doubte ye not that god punyssheth you for thynobedyence that ye doo to your fader and to your moder/ wherfore I praye you fayre Vyenne to telle to me for what cause ye wyl not haue me in maryage to your husbond/ Doubte ye that whan ye shall be wyth me/ that ye may not serue god as wel as ye now do that suffre thys payne/ I promyse you by my fayth þ^t ye shal haue playsaunces and lybertees in al the maners that ye shal conne demaunde/ Thenne I praye you [dj^r] that ye wyl not here deye so dolor- ously/ and yf ye wyl not doo it for the loue of me/ yet at the leste do it for the loue of your fader and of your moder whyche lyue for you in grete sorowe and in grete heuynesse/ wherfore ye ought to haue pyte on them/

Whan Vyenne had herde these wordes she was quasi abasshed and sayd syr sauyng your honour I am maryed/ how be it ye knowe hym not whome I haue in myn hert/ And also I knowe and graunte ryght wel that ye be worthy to haue one moche gretter and more hye a lady than I am/ and I late you wete that for hym that I desyre I shold suffre more payne than I fele/ And therfore I praye you that fro hens forth ye speke to me no more of thys mater/ And also I am so euyl dysposed in my persone that yf it endure in me/ my lyf shal not be longe/ and yf it were honeste I shold shewe it you and than shold ye see how it stondeth wyth me/ Neuertheles approche ye ner to me/ & ye shall the better byleue me/ And the sone of the duke of bourgoyne & the bysshop of saynt laurence approuched vnto vyenne/ fro whom yssued soo grete a stenche/ that vnnethe they myght suffre and endure it/ whiche sauour came fro vnder hyr arme holes of the two quarters of the henne/ whiche were roten/ And whan vyenne sawe that they had felte ynough of the stenche

she sayd to them/ lordes ye may now knowe ynough in what
aduenture I am dysposed/ Thenne they took leue hauyng
grete compassyon on hyr/ And they sayd to the dolphyn
that vyenne was thenne half roten and that she stanke/ and
demed in them self that she myght not lyue longe/ and that 5
it shold be grete damage of hyr deth for the souerayn beaute
that was in hyr/ And Incontynent the sone of the duc of
bourgoyn took hys leue of the doulphyn/ and retorned in
to hys contrey/ and recounted to hys fader the lyf of vyenne/
wherof alle they that herde hym had grete pyte in theyr 10
herte/

Whan the doulphyn sawe that the maryage was broken/
by the deffaulte of his doughter Vyenne/ he sware that
she shold neuer departe fro thens/ but yf she wold
consente to hys wylle/ 15

And so she abode longe tyme in that pryson where she had
grete thought and sorowe for hyr swete and trewe frende
parys/ & hyr desyre was on noo thyng but for to here tydynges
of parys hyr loue/ But in the estate [dj^v] that she was in/ no
man myght brynge hyr tydynges/ And Edward the felowe of 20
Parys seyng that Vyenne abode in soo grete payne/ and that
none durst speke to hyr/ he had in hys herte grete sorowe/ &
was moche moeued of grete pyte/ and also for the grete loue
that he had to parys/ And concluded to make a chapel in the
chyrche that touched the palays of the dolphyn and in a corner 25
he dyd do dygge so depe that it was nyghe to the foundement
of the pryson/ wherein vyenne was/ and by cause he wold not
haue the thyng dysclosed/ he wold that they shold dygge no
ferther/ and whan the chapel was achyeued and fynysshed/
Edward alle allone dygged hym self so ferre/ that he made an 30
hole/ by whyche he spake to vyenne whan he wold whyche
caue was made so secretly that no man myȝt apperceyue it/
Soo it happed on a day Edward byhelde vyenne thurgh this
hole/ & salewed hyr/ & thenne whan vyenne herd hym &
knewe hym/ she had so grete Ioye & consolacyon/ that she 35
semed that she was rysen fro deth to lyf/ & the fyrst tydynges
that Vyenne demaunded of hym were yf he knewe ony

[Paris and Vienne]

tydynges of parys & edward tolde to hir that it was not longe
syth/ that he had receyued a letter fro hym/ wryton at genes/
Thenne said vyenne al wepyng to hym/ alas whan shal þe day
come that I shal see hym/ & that doon I wold be contente
that god shold do his wylle of me/ for none other thyng I
desyre in this world/ Alas fayr brother what semeth you of
my lyf & of this fayr chambre in whyche I dwelle in/ certeynly
I byleue veryly/ that yf parys knewe it/ þt for his loue I suffre
thus moche sorowe/ that the hert of hym shold swelte for
sorowe/ and after she tolde to Edward the parlament that she
had with the sone of the duc of bourgoyne/ & also of the
henne/ & prayed hym þt he wold sende worde of al thys to
parys & that she recommaunded hyr to hym/ & also that she
had none other hope in thys world but in hym/ Edward
brought to hyr euery day fro thenne forthon mete & drynke/
& al that was necessarye to hyr/ for hyr lyf/ & comforted hyr
with fayr wordes the best wyse he myght/ & Edward wrote
al playnly to parys/ how for hungre she shold haue been dede/
ne had he ben/ whyche dayly pourueyed for hyr al that was
to hym necessarye/ and he wrote to hym alle the manere that
Vyenne had holden wyth the sone of the Duke of Bourgoyne
And that thys fayre lady Vyenne desyred noo thynge in
this world but for to see hym onely [dij^r] And also that she
prayed hym that he shold not departe oute of the contree
that he was in/

Whan the noble Parys had receyued the letter fro
Edward and knewe that vyenne abode in pryson/ it
is no nede to demaunde yf he had grete desplaysyr[1]/ &
almoost was in suche caas/ as to lese his wytte for sorowe/ And
on that other parte he had grete drede that she shold be
maryed in eschewyng of the grete harme & payne that she
suffred/ and herein he was pensyf nyght and day/ sayeng to
hym self/ I see wel that I may not escape but that vyenne
must nedes be maryed/ and by that moyen hyr loue and myn
shal faylle/ Alas now see I wel that now me byhoueth noo
hoope ne truste/ Alas caytyf and vnhappy what shal byfalle

---
[1] despaysyr C.

of me/ I shal goo so ferre/ that fro hyr I may neuer here tydynges/ ne also she fro me/ and after this he bygan ageyn hys complaynte sayeng/ O veray god of heuen wherfore hast thou not doon to me soo moche grace/ that in the stede of hyr I myght suffre the payne that she suffreth for me/ ¶O cruel fortune ful of cruel tormente/ and what hath vyenne doon or made that she must suffre so greuous penaunce/ Alas were it not more reason/ Iustyce and cause that I whyche haue doon alle thys euyl bere the punycyon/ certes yes/

¶ *How Parys sente a letter to Edward hys felowe/*

After that he had made hys complaynte/ he wrote a letter vnto Edward/ doyng hym to wyte how he had souerayn sorowe for vyenne whiche was in pryson/ and he thanked hym of the goodnes and dylygence that he had doon toward hyr/ in prayeng hym that he neuer wold faylle hyr/ but contynuelly ayde and helpe hyr/ ¶And after he wrote to hym how for veray dysplaysyr and melancolye he wold goo in to somme straunge contreye/ And that fro than forthon he shold sende to hym noo moo letters/ And that he neuer retche for to here moo tydynges fro hym/ nomore than of a deed persone/ ¶Thenne whan Edward had receyued these letters fro Paris and knewe that he wold estraunge hym fro that contree of genes/ and wold goo in to a strange contreye he was moche wroth and sore agryeued/

¶And thenne Incontynent edward[1] wente and tolde it to the fader and moder of Parys [dij^v] wherof they toke so grete sorowe that they supposed to haue loste theyr wytte/ And after edward wente and tolde it also to vyenne/ wherof it nedeth not to demaunde the grete sorowe that she had/ for it was so grete and ouermoche/ that yf edward had not comforted hyr/ she had been dede/ And thenne she complayned to ysabeau sayeng that sythen she neuer entended to here tydynges of hyr loue Parys she was ryght wel contente to deye and that she wold neuer more haue playsyr of no thynge that

[1] parys C.

[Paris and Vienne] 59

was in thys world/ and that thenne she wold that she were
dede/ And ysabeau comforted hyr alwaye

¶ *How parys wente to shyppe at venyse/ for to goo to the holy
sepulcre in Iherusalem/*

After that paris had sent the letter to Edward Incontynent he departed fro genes wyth hys seruaunte/ and
wente to venyse where he took shyppyng/ and saylled 5
so ferre that he cam to alexandrye/ where he abode a space of
tyme/ & after in that contrey he enformed hym & lerned the
waye to the mounte of caluarye and of Iherusalem/ and how
he myght passe surely/ And afterward Parys concluded to goo
in to that contrey a pylgrymage/ but tofore or he took hys 10
waye/ he lerned for to speke the langage of moores/ And whan
Parys coude wel speke mouryske/ he and his varlet took the
waye toward ynde/ Ande so ferre laboured by theyr Iourneyes/
that they arryued in the londe of prester Iohan/ In whyche
he dwelled a longe tyme And in that whyle hys berde grewe 15
longe/ and after he took the habyte of a more/ and also lerned
alle the custommes and maners of the contree/ And he had
alle waye faste byleue in our lord Ihesu Cryste/ and in the
gloryous vyrgyn marye hys swete moder/ And thus abydyng
in thys maner he had grete wylle to goo to Iherusalem to 20
the holy sepulture/ for to see the holy sayntuaryes/ & for
taccomplysshe the holy pylgremage/ Thenne whan he was in
Iherusalem/ he sette al his courage in deuocyon/ & bycam so
deuoute that it was meruaylle/ and prayed contynuelly our
lord that by the meryte of his passyon he wold gyue to hym 25
saluacyon of hys soule/ & consolacyon for his body & also for
fayr vyenne/ & after he departed fro thens and wente in to
Egypte/ and arryued in the contree of the soudan/ & hys
money bygan to faylle/ & hyred hym a litel hous wherin he
dwellyd moche heuy and sorouful [diij^r] for hys Infortune/ 30
And also he had grete desplaysyr whan he sawe other tryumphe
and wexe lordes/ Now it happed on a day that parys wente to
playe and dysporte hym out of the toun in the feldes/ and

[*Paris and Vienne*]

there mette with the faulconners of the soudan/ whyche came fro hawkyng/ and emonge them was one fawcon moche seke/ and that fawcon the sowdan loued beste of alle the other/ Thenne demaunded Parys of the fawconner what sekenesse the fawcon had/ And the fawconner sayd to hym that he 5 wyst not/ Thenne sayd paris truly yf he contynue in the maladye that he hath he shall not lyue thre dayes/ but yf ye doo that I shal say to you/ and yf he be not hole therwyth he shal neuer be hole/ Thenne sayd þe fawlconner to hym/ I praye you that ye wyl telle me what I shal do for I ensure 10 you faythfully/ that yf ye may make hym hole/ it shal mowe auaylle you and me also and that I promyse you/ for the souldan had leuer lose the beste cyte that he hath than this fawcon/ Thenne Parys wente and sought certayn herbes/ and gaf them to the fawlconner and bad hym to bynde them to 15 the feet of the fawcon/ and so he dyd/ and sone after the fawlcon amended and becam as hole as euer he had be tofore/ wherof þe souldan was moche Ioyous/ and for loue of thys faulcon/ the souldan made the fawlconner a grete lord[1] in hys courte/ Thenne the faulconner seyng that by the moyen of 20 parys he had goten thys lordshyp/ he dyd to hym moche playsyr/ & shewed to hym as grete amytye and frendshyp as he[2] had ben hys brother/ & brought hym in the grace of the souldan/ and was receyued in to hys courte/ & the souldan loued hym soo wel/ that he gaf to hym grete offyce/ and 25 mayntened hym in grete honour/ ye shal vnderstonde that in thys tyme regned a moche holy pope/ the whych was named Innocent/ and was a moche holy persone & deuoute/ And it plesed soo hym that he gaf oute a croysee/ ayenst the fals myscreauntes & hethen men/ to the ende that the name of 30 our lord Ihesu cryst were more sayntefyed and enhaunced thurgh out al crystyente/ And therfore was maad a grete counceyl emonge the cardynals and prelates/ & was concluded by theyr parlament that thys croysee shold be wryton to the kyng of fraunce/ and to other kynges crysten/ dukes/ Erles 35 and other grete lordes/ and so was it doon/

[1] serd C.   [2] be C.

[Paris and Vienne] 61

¶ *How the doulphyn came toward the kyng of Fraunce/* [diij^v]

Whan the kyng of france had receyued the letters fro the pope/ Incontynent he sente for the doulphyn of vyennoys/ that he shold come and speke wyth hym/ the whiche Incontynent came at his commaundement/ Thenne the kynge sayd to hym/ Syr Godefroy/ we haue made you to 5
come hyther/ for ye be one of þ^e moost wysest of our courte/ & also ye be of our lygnage/ And we late you wete that our holy fader the pope hath wryton to vs that he hath yeuen a croysee ayenst the mescreauntes wherfore we for the loue and reuerence of god entende for to goo thyder/ Neuertheles we 10
haue aduysed/ that ye shold goo fyrst in to thoo partyes/ & we praye you for the loue and reuerence of god that ye take on you the charge for to espye the contrees and also the passages/ Thenne the doulphyn sayd/ I am redy & apparaylled to do your comaundement wyth good wylle/ But how shal I 15
mowe doo it for to passe surely emonge the hethen peple/ For yf they apperceyue in ony wyse that I goo for to espye theyr contree/ I shal not conne escape/ But that I must deye by cruel deth yf god kepe me not/ Thenne sayd the kyng ye may goo and your companye surely clothed in habyte of pylgryms/ 20
for ye knowe wel that thys is not the fyrst tyme/ that many crysten men haue been in the holy londe/ wherfor I praye you yet eft ones that in þ^e name of Ihesu cryst that ye make you redy for to goo thyder/ and take wyth you of our knyghtes as meny as it shal playse you/ 25

¶ Thenne the doulphyn seyng the wylle of the kyng/ and that Incontynent he must departe/ he sente letters to hys wyf/ that he wold goo in to the holy londe to seche the holy sayntuaryes & pylgrymages/ and prayed hyr that she moche wysely shold gouerne hys londe/ & that vyenne hys doughter 30
shold not escape oute of pryson tyl he retourned for in shorte tyme he wold come ageyn/

[Paris and Vienne]

¶ *How the Doulphyn took hys shyppyng for to goo in to Iherusalem/*

After that the doulphyn had taken hys shyppe & passed in to Surrye and damaske/ to Iherusalem and in many other places/ & had aduysed and espyed moche wysely and wel alle the contree/ And enquyred of the crysten men that dwellyd there many thynges/ without dyscoueryng his wylle and entente/ Neuertheles somme euyl crysten men for to gete money tolde it vnto the souldan of [d iiij^r] babylone/ ¶ Thenne whan the souldan knewe it/ he maad noo semblaunte/ but Incontynent he made all the passages to be kept where as the pylgryms went by in suche manere as the doulphyn was taken & alle hys companye wyth hym in a place called Ramon not ferre fro Iherusalem/ whyche was brought tofore the souldan/ and he ordeyned that the doulphyn shold be tormented and pyned/ The doulphyn seyng hym self in suche a poynte sayd that they shold not tormente hym/ and he wold say to them the trouthe/ & thus he recounted to the souldan how the Pope had gyuen oute a croysee ayenst them/ & how he was comen to espye the contreye/ whan the souldan sawe thys/ he sayd that he wold aduyse hym of what deth he wold do hym to deth/ in maner that al other shold take ensaumple/ And commaunded that anone he shold be ledde in to alysandrye/ & there to be put in to an harde pryson/ and also that none shold gyue to hym but brede and water/ Thenne the doulphyn was brought in to Alysandrye/ & was put in to an hard and stronge toure/ & there he suffred a myserable lyf/ and had kepars that kept hym ny3t and day/ Thus was the doulphyn in grete sorowe/ thynkyng neuer to yssue out of þ^t pryson but dede/ Neuertheles the Pope and the kyng of Fraunce dyd ofte tymes grete payne to haue hym out by fynaunces/ but they myght not haue hym/ ¶ For the souldan sayd that he shold do on hym suche punycyon/ that al other shold take ensaumple/ Now late vs leue to speke of the doulphyn/ and retorne we to Parys that knewe no thynge of these tydynges

[Paris and Vienne]

Now recounteth thystorye that parys was in babylone lyke as ye haue tofore herde/ whyche knewe noo thynge of thys fayte/ So it happed that by aduenture ij freres relygyous sought thyndulgences of the holy lande & aryueden in babylone/ where they wold see the seygnorye & the puyssaunce of the sowdan/ For thenne the sowdan helde hym in Babylone wyth moche grete puyssaunce/ These two freres were of these partyes/ whyche beyng in tho partyes it happed as they wente in the towne parys fonde them/ Thenne parys salewed them & demaunded of these partyes and sayd to them in thys manere/ After that I haue herde say emonge you crysten men ye haue a Pope/ the whyche is moche stronge & puyssaunt/ And also ye haue many kynges/ & grete lordes/ & so grete townes cytees [diiij^v] and castellys/ that I haue merueyll how he suffre that we that be not of your lawe haue the seygnorye of the holy lande whiche ought to apperteyne to you as ye say/ And whan the freres had herde Parys thus speke/ they were sore aferde/ And one of them ansuerd in the langage of moure/ For they wyst none other but parys was a moure/ & so dyd al they of the contrey/ & he sayd to hym/ Syr I byleue wel that ye haue herd say/ that in our partyes been assembled grete companyes of peple & men of warre for to come in to thyse partyes/ by cause that our holy fader the Pope/ hath graunted oute a croysee/ and in the tyme whyles our men of warre assembled/ the kynge of fraunce whiche is the grettest of crystyente/ sente a noble baron whyche is named the doulphyn of vyennoys for to vysyte and espye these partyes/ Thenne he beyng in these partyes/ the souldan sette men in suche places where as the pylgryms were accustomed to passe/ And sodeynly he dyd do take hym in a cyte named Ramon/ and after sente hym in to Alysandrye/ and there sette hym in an euyl pryson/ wherein I suppose that he be dede/ and thus for thys cause/ the fayt was dyscouerd/ Thenne sayd Parys how is that lord named/ Thenne sayd the frere/ he is named godefroy of Allaunson doulphyn of vyennoys/ And whan parys herde thys he was moche abasshed/ but he made noo semblaunter/ And thought in hys hert/ that hys aduenture myght yet come to good and effecte/ Thenne

64   [*Paris and Vienne*]

he demaunded them of many thynges/ and sayd to them/ that
he wold more speke to them another tyme/ and demaunded
them where they were lodged/ and they tolde hym more for
drede than for loue/ for they thought he wold haue doon to
them somme harme/   5

Whan Parys was departed fro the freres/ he was moche
pensyf how and in what maner he myght goo in to
Alexandrye for to see the doulphyn/ & how he myght
gete hym oute of pryson/ and so moche he thought on his
fayte/ that he purposed to goo to the hostry where the freres 10
were lodged/ and soo wente thyder/ & whan the freres sawe
hym/ they were sore aferde Thenne parys took them by the
handes/ and ladde them to solace thurgh þᵉ cyte spekyng of
many thynges alwaye in the langage of moure/ & sayd to
them/ I haue grete desyre to see that crysten knyght whiche 15
is in alexandrye For I haue alwaye had good wylle to the
crysten men/ peraduenture I myght yet wel helpe [dvʳ] hym/
& yf ye wyl come with me I promyse you by my lawe/ that
I shal make you good chere/ & doubte ye nothyng/ and thenne
whan the freres herde hym thus speke they wyst not what to 20
ansuer/ they had so grete fere/ Neuertheles they trustyng in
the mercy of god/ they promysed hym/ that they shold goo
wyth hym/ though they shold deye/ & prayden god in theyr
courage that he wold graunte grace that he myght come oute
of pryson/ Thenne Parys had grete playsyr of the ansuer of 25
the freres & wende neuer to see þᵉ houre/ that he myght be
wyth the doulphyn for to see the ende of his aduenture/ and
so departed fro the freres/ and wente strayte to the faulconner
of the souldan wyth whom he had grete knowleche/ & sayd
to hym/ Seynour I thanke you of the grete honour/ curtosye 30
& gentylnes that ye haue do to me/ & playse it you to wyte
that I wyl departe fro hens in to alysandrye/ and I promyse
to you that for your loue I shall not tarye longe/ but that
I shal retorne hyther ageyn/ And by cause I am there vn-
knowen/ and that I neuer was there/ I praye you ryght 35
humbly/ that I myʒt haue a maundement of the souldan/ that
he commaunde to the gouernours that I may goo thorugh alle

[*Paris and Vienne*] 65

hys londe surely / For ye knowe wel that one may not kepe
hym ouer wel fro euyl peple / Therfore I praye you and requyre
that ye wyl gete me suche a maundement / and also that ye
wyl commaunde me humbly to the good grace of my lord the
souldan / and forthwyth the faulconner wente to the souldan
and made hys requeste for Parys / & Incontynent the souldan
graunted hym al hys desyre / sayeng that it moche desplaysed
hym / of the departyng of parys & yf he wold abyde & dwelle
in hys courte he wold make hym a grete lord / Thenne the
faulconner sayd / Dere syr he hath promysed me / that in short
tyme he shal retorne / Thenne the souldan dyd do make the
maundement lyke as he wold deuyse / chargyng al his lordes
offycers & subgettes of townes cytees & castellys of his londe
that they shold do to hym grete honour / & that they shold
gyue & delyuer to hym al that shold be necessarye to hym
wythout takyng ony money or ony other thynge of hym / And
also the souldan gaf to Parys many ryche clothes & vestymentes of cloth of gold and of sylke / and also he gaf to hym
grete tresour / prayeng hym that he shold not longe tarye / but
hastely retorne ageyn / & promysed hym that he shold make
hym a grete lord / and delyuerd hys [d v^v] maundement / the
whyche was sealed wyth the proper seale of the souldan / and
sygned wyth hys owne hande

Whan Parys had receyued alle these thynges that the
souldan had gyuen to hym / he took leue of hym and
of hys courte & went with the freres in to Alexandrye /
Incontynent after he was comen he shewed the maundement
to the admyral / the whyche anon after he had seen it dyd
grete honour to Parys / and delyuerd to hym a fayr lodgyng
pourueyed of al thynges necessarye / and delyuerd another to
the freres / Thadmyral came euery day to see parys in hys
lodgyng for to do hym honour and companye / and wente &
rode to gyder thorugh the cyte / and by cause that Parys was
rychely clad / euery man made to hym grete honour and sayd
that he semed wel to be the sone of somme grete moure And
on a day as they rode in the cyte they passed forth by the
toure where as the dolphyn was in pryson / ¶ Thenne Parys

[*Paris and Vienne*]

demaunded of the admyral what toure it was that was so
fayre/ Thenne he tolde to hym þ{t} it was a moche cruel pryson
& terryble In whyche the souldan helde a prysonner a grete
lord & baron of the[1] weste[1]/ whyche was comen for tespye
these contreyes/ Thenne sayd parys I praye you late vs goo
see hym/ & the admyral sayd he shold gladly/ Thenne they
alyghted fro their horses/ & entred in to the pryson/ and whan
parys sawe the doulphyn/ he had in hys hert grete desplaysyr/
by cause of the myserable & sorouful lyf that he suffred/ &
Parys demaunded of þ{e} kepars what man he was/ And they
sayd/ that he was a grete baron of Fraunce/ Thenne sayd
parys/ vnderstondeth he mourysshe/ and they sayd nay/ but
that notwythstondyng yf he wold speke to hym/ that they
shold fynde tourchemen ynough/ Thenne sayd Parys he wold
retorne another day for to demaunde of hym of the partyes
of the weste/ & prayed thadmyral to gyue comandement to
the kepars/ that as ofte as he shold come/ that they shold
shewe hym to hym/ & Incontynent he comanded lyke as parys
had desyred/ & thenne they departed/ & a fewe dayes after
parys retorned and came to the pryson and brought one of
the freres wyth hym that coude speke mouryske/ & whan they
were wythin the pryson/ paris sayd to the frere that he shold
salewe hym curtoysly/ Neuertheles the frere knewe noo thynge
that parys coude speke frensshe/ Thenne the frere sayd to the
doulphyn/ that that lord was come [d vj{r}] for to vysyte hym/
& that he loued wel crysten men/ & that he was wel in the
grace of the souldan/ and that he trusted ys moche in hym as
in ony man of hys contreye/ & thus the frere demaunded many
thynges of the doulphyn in the name of parys/ and sayd yf he
myght doo for hym he wold gladly

Whan the doulphyn herde the relygious frere thus speke
in the persone of the moure/ he was moche abasshed
in hys courage/ bysechyng our lord that he wold put
hym in suche courage & good wylle for to brynge hym out of
pryson Parys desyred to here tydynges of the fayr vyenne
sayd to the frere/ that he shold aske of the doulphyn yf he

[1] theste C.

[Paris and Vienne] 67

had ony wyf or chyldren/ Thenne the dolphyn began to wepe/
& said that he had a wyf/ & a doughter holden for the fayrest
of Fraunce/ whom he helde in pryson bycause she wold take
noo husbond/ Thenne paris began to comforte hym by the
mouthe of the frere/ sayeng that he shold take alle in pacyence/ 5
& god shold yet ones delyuer hym oute of pryson/ by whyche
wordes the doulphyn was so reioyced & Ioyous/ that hym
semed that god had appyered to hym/ & the doulphyn sayd
to the frere that it was grete pyte that the moure was not
crysten/ & prayed our lord that he wold gyue to hym puys- 10
saunce to kepe hym in that good wylle that he had & so
departed that one fro that other moche comforted/ Thenne
parys sayd to the kepars that he had founde so grete playsyr
in the prysonner/ that he wold ofte tymes come for to dysporte
hym and they sayd whan it playsed hym he shold retorne 15
& be welcome/ and thenne parys sayd to the freres that were
in þ^t place yf I thought to be sure of you/ I thynke wel to
fynde the moyen to brynge thys prysonner out of pryson/ &
the freres were moche admerueylled of thys whiche parys had
sayd to them/ and they sayd to hym/ by the fayth that we 20
owe to our god/ that of vs ye nede not to doubte/ & in caas
that ye be in wylle late vs assaye but it must be doon secretely/
for ye see wel how many kepars been there contynuelly/
Thenne sayd Parys I shal gyue to you good counceyl and
remedye of alle thys/ but I wyl haue two thynges/ The fyrst 25
thynge is I wyl that ye goo wyth me/ That other is that he
shal gyue to me my lyuyng honourably in hys contre/ for I
am in grete doubte whan I haue delyuerd hym/ and shal be
in hys contreye that he wyl sette nought by me/ and I can
noo mestyer ne crafte/ and [d vj^v] soo I myght be wel deceyued/ 30
Therfore yf he wyl assure me/ & that he wyl gyue to me a yefte
suche as I shal demaunde hym whan I shal be in hys contreye/
I shal delyuer hym & shal leue my contree for loue of hym/ &
ye may see in what estate I am/

[*Paris and Vienne*]

On the morne Parys and the freres came in to the pryson & the frere recounted al thys to the doulphyn/ & whan the doulphyn vnderstood thys/ hym thought that god bare hym awaye/ & sayd/ I thanke god & thys moure of the good wylle that he hath toward me/ For I neuer dyd hym 5 seruyce ne playsyr wherfore he ought to do so moche for me/ Neuertheles I hope that is the playsyr of god that he shal delyuer me oute of pryson/ I am redy to swere vpon the body of Ihesu Cryst or I euer departe from hens/ that assone as I shal be in myn owne lande I shal mayntene hym in more 10 gretter estate/ than he ne is here and I wyl that he doo alle hys wylle of al my londe/ for it shal suffyse to me onely that I haue a lyuyng for me and my wyf/ and I shal do al that he wylle/ and so say ye to hym on my behalue/ And thenne the frere tolde al to parys that whych the doulphyn had sayd 15 and promysed to do/ and to thende that parys shold be more sure/ he sayd to the frere that he shold brynge tofore hym the body of our lord Ihesu cryst/ and that tofore hym he shold swere to holde alle that he promysed/ and the frere tolde it to Parys/ and the doulphyn sware it tofore Parys to accom- 20 plysshe alle that he had promysed And whan he had sworne/ to the ende that Parys shold be the better contente/ the doulphyn receyued the precyous body of our lord Ihesu Cryst/ sayeng that it shold be to the dampnacyon of hys soule/ in caas that he accomplysshed not al that he had 25 promysed whan they shold be in his londe/ and whan thys was doo parys and the freres departed fro the doulphyn/ and wente to the porte/ for to wyte yf there were ony fuste that wold come hytherward/ and by aduenture they fonde a fuste/ and Parys wyth the freres spake to the patrone and promysed 30 hym a M besaunts of gold yf they wold lete haue passage fyue persones/ The Patron seyng the grete tresour/ sayd to them that he was contente/ but he wold haue half at the porte/ and sayd to them/ lordes I praye you make you redy/ for in caas that the moures of thys londe fonde vs we shold be al 35 dede/ ¶Thenne sayd Parys make your self al redy/ for thys nyght at mydnyght I [ejʳ] shal come/ And after thys Parys retorned to hys lodgyng & dyd do make redy moche vytayll

[Paris and Vienne] 69

and the best wynes that he coude gete & he with the
freres maad prouysyon of alle other thynges and mantellys
and towellys/

Whan al was redy parys wente to the kepars of the
pryson and sayd/ I thanke you many tymes of the
playsyrs that ye haue doon to me/ I wyl now departe
fro hens for to retorne to my lord the souldan/ but for your
loue I wyl soupe wyth you thys nyght and praye yow that
we may soupe to gyder/ & they ansuerd that it wel pleased
them for his loue Thenne Parys sente for the vytayll & for
the wyn /and after it was come/ they souped to gyder/ And
the kepars which had not been accustomed to drynke wyn/
dranke so moche that they alle were dronke/ & Incontynent
leyed them doun to slepe/ & slepte so faste/ that for noo
thyng they coude not awake them/ & whan parys sawe that/
he sayd to the freres/ that they shold vnfeter the doulphyn/ &
that they shold opene the yates of the pryson/ & yf ony of
the kepars awake I shal slee hym/ Thenne the freres began
to vnfetere the doulphyn wyth grete drede/ prayeng god to
be theyr ayde and helpe/ And whan the doulphyn was loos
he cladde hym lyke a moure After Parys slewe alle the kepars
one after another by cause yf they awoke they shold not
come after them/

Thys doon/ the doulphyn wyth parys and his varlet/ and
the two freres camen to the porte/ and hastely entred in
to the fuste which was al redy/ and wonde vp theyr
saylle/ and by the helpe of god began so fast to saylle that
wythin fewe dayes they arryueden in a place that thenne was
crysten and there the doulphyn wente a londe by cause he
was moche greued and annoyed as wel of the see/ as for the
harme that he had suffred in pryson/ and there borowed
money/ and fro thens came in to cypres/ where was a kyng
whyche had dwellyd in the courte of the kyng of fraunce
The whiche as sone as he knewe that the doulphyn of vyennoys
was come/ he went to mete hym and prayed hym that he
wold come and lodge in hys paleys/ And the doulphyn wente

[*Paris and Vienne*]

thyder/ wherof the kyng had grete Ioye/ & there he made hym
grete chyere/ for many tymes they had seen eche other in þe
kynges court of Fraunce/ and after the kyng demaunded hym
of his aduenture/ & the doulphyn recounted [ej^v] it to hym
al alonge/ and bycause of the comyng of the doulphyn he 5
made moche grete feste/ and receyued hym moche hyely/ and
made hym to soiourne there as longe as it playsed hym/ And
whan the doulphyn had soiourned there at his playsyr/ he
took leue of the kyng and of al hys courte/ thankyng hym
moche of the grete playsyr þ^t he had doon to hym/ The kyng 10
seyng that the doulphyn wold departe/ he gaf to hym grete
yeftes/ and dyd do arme two galleyes whyche accompanyed
hym/ and brought hym vpon the see/ and had soo good wynde
that in fewe dayes after they brought hym in to aygues
mortes/ 15

Whan the doulphyn was arryued/ the knyghtes of the
doulphyne herde it anone/ and forthwyth maad them
redy & went to horsback & mette wyth hym at aygues
mortes/ & there receyued hym in grete honour/ & so came
forth the ry3t waye to vyenne/ and for Ioye of hys comyng/ al 20
they of the cyte made a moche noble and meruayllous feste/
whyche endured wel fyftene dayes/ & the playsyr & Ioye was
so grete emonge them by cause they had recouuerd theyr
lord/ that noo man shold and coude haue thought it/ Parys
in alle this wyse neuer chaunged hys vesture ne clothyng but 25
contynuelly wente to masse/ and by the commaundement of
the doulphyn the people dyd hym grete reuerence & honour/
so moche that parys was ashamed therof/ and spake noo
thynge but mouryske/ And he had a grete berde/ and made
to noo persone of the world ony knowleche/ and after a 30
whyle of tyme/ the doulphyn for taccomplysshe that he had
promysed to parys by the frere/ dyd do say to parys and do
demaunde yf he wold haue the seygnourye of hys londe and
contree/ For he was al redy for taccomplysshe that/ whyche
he had promysed/ And Parys made to hym ansuer/ that he 35
shold kepe stylle hys londe/ Thenne the doulphyn dyd
demaunde hym yf he wold haue hys doughter vyenne/ and

[*Paris and Vienne*] 71

parys made the frere to say ye/ for that pleased hym wel/ And
thenne they wente to hyr/
¶ Thenne whan they were tofore Vyenne the frere spake first
Madame ye knowe wel that my lord your fader hath ben a
grete whyle in pryson/ and yet shold haue been/ ne had haue 5
been/ thys moure/ whyche hath saued hym/ puttyng hys
persone in ryght grete peryl and daunger for the loue of my
lord your fader/ And thus ye may wel [e ij^r] knowe how moche
he is holden to hym/ & by cause herof your fader is subget to
hym euer/ wherfore your fader prayeth you that vpon al the 10
playsyr that ye wyl doo for hym/ that ye wyll take hym for
your husbond/ And he shal pardonne all the desplaysyr that
euer ye dyd to hym/ whan the frere had fynysshed his wordes/
vyenne ansuerd to hym sayeng/ The bysshop of saynt laurence
knoweth wel that is here present that it is longe syth that yf 15
I wold haue be maryed/ I myght haue ben maryed wyth more
honour vnto my fader/ than vnto this moure/ for the sone of
the duc of borgoyne had espoused me yf I wold haue consented
but god hath put me in suche a maladye/ that I may not longe
lyue in this world/ & euery day my maladye encreaceth & so 20
enpayreth me that I am half roten wherfor I praye you to say
to my fader that he holde me excused/ for at thys tyme I wyl
not be maryed/ Thenne they took theyr leue of vyenne &
recounted alle thys to the doulphyn/ Thenne the doulphyn
sayd to the frere that he shold say it to the moure/ & so the 25
frere tolde it al to parys/ and thenne parys which was aferde
to lese the loue of vyenne/ wente for to see hyr in the pryson
with the frere & the bysshop of saynt laurence/ Thenne whan
Parys sawe vyenne in that dysposycyon/ he had moche grete
sorowe & grete merueylle/ and thenne he made the frere to 30
salewe hyr in hys name/ and vyenne ansuerd vnto hys gretyng
ryght curtoysly/ & the frere sayd in the name of parys/
Madame ye knowe wel I haue delyuerd your fader oute of
pryson/ wherof ye ought to haue synguler playsyr/ & yet he
shold haue been there yf I had not haue been and holpen 35
hym oute/ & he pardonneth you with good hert and good
wylle alle the desplaysyrs that euer ye dyd ageynst hys
playsyr/ And prayeth you that ye take me for your husbond/

and wyll that we haue the lordshyp of the doulphyne/ and
therfor I praye you/ that neyther ye nor I lose not thys
honour/ ¶And yet more though thys were not/ ye ought not
to dysobeye the commaundementes of your fader/ ¶And
thenne vyenne ansuerd to the frere as to the persone of Parys 5
sayeng/ I knowe well that ye haue delyuerd my fader oute of
pryson/ not wythstondyng my fader shal haue suche regarde
ageynst you that ye shal lese noo thynge/ ¶And I wote wel
that ye be a man of grete lygnage/ & are worthy[1] to haue a
gretter lady than I am/ But the bysshop of seynt Laurence 10
whyche is present knoweth [e ij^v] wel that for the maladye
that I am in/ I may not longe lyue/ & thenne sayd the frere
in his name this is by cause I am a moure that ye refuse me/
I promyse you that I shal become crysten/ but I thynke wel
that yf ye knewe who that I am/ and what I haue lefte for to 15
brynge your fader oute of pryson/ that ye wold preyse me
more than ye doo/ knowe ye for certeyn that your fader shal
be pariured/ for he hath promysed that ye shal be my wyf
wherof ye shal haue blame/ therfore yf it playse you graunte
ye hym hys wylle/ Thenne sayd vyenne/ lord I haue herd say 20
moche good of you/ & that ye be he that haue doon so moche
for my fader/ but neuertheles in the maladye in the whyche
I am/ none ought to counceyl me to take an husbond/ For
my lyf may not longe endure/ and by cause that ye may
knowe that I say trouth approche ye ner to me/ & ye shal fele 25
and smelle in what dysposycyon I am of my persone/ And
thenne they approuched ner to hyr/ and vyenne had put two
quarters of an henne vnder hyr two arme hooles/ and there
yssued so grete stenche that the bysshop ne the frere myght
not suffre it/ Neuertheles the stynche was to parys a good 30
odour/ for he smellyd it not & sayd I wote not what ye
smelle/ for I fele none euyl sauour/ And they meruaylled
strongely/ by cause he felte not the odour/ And the frere sayd
in parys name/ For this odour shal I neuer leue you & I
assure you I shal neuer departe fro hens vntyl ye haue con- 35
sented to that your fader wyl/ and vyenne answerd moche
angrely & sayd by the fayth that I owe to god I shal rather

[1] thorthy C.

[Paris and Vienne]

renne wyth my hede ayenst the walle that I shal make my
brayn yssue oute of my mouth/ & so shal ye be the occasyon
of my dethe/ Thenne sayd the frere ye shal not so doo madame/
For I promyse you fro hens forth/ that I shal neuer speke
more to you/ sythe that it is not your wylle ne plesyr/ but 5
atte leste of one thyng I praye you/ that this nyght ye aduyse
you/ and I shal retorne to morn for to haue of you an ansuer/
and ye shal take counceyll of your felowe/ and I praye to god
that ye may be wel counceylled/ and alle these thynges sayd
the frere in the name of parys to vyenne/ And after they took 10
theyr leue of vyenne/ and sayd alle to the doulphyn/ wherof
he was thenne moche dyspleased/ and bad the frere to telle
it alle vnto Parys for to excuse hym/ and that he shold not
leye the blame on hym/ ¶And whan they were departed fro
vyenne/ she sayd to ysabeau/ My [e iij^r] fayr suster/ what 15
semeth you of the wysedom of my fader/ that thynketh that
I shold take thys moure to my husbond/ and haue refused
the sone of the Duke of bourgoyne/ but god forbede that euer
in my lyf I haue other lord than Parys to myn husbond/
whome I hope yet to haue/ & ysabeau sayd/ Certes Madame 20
I wote not what to say of your fader whyche wold gyue you
to a moure in maryage/ I haue therof grete thought/ for he
hath sayd that he shal retorne to morn to see you/ and hath
sayd that ye shold remembre and aduyse you/

¶ *How Parys came to see vyenne in the pryson/ and how she
knewe hym/*

And on the morn betymes Parys cladde hym moche more 25
rychely than he had be accustomed/ & gyrde wyth a
moche ryche swerde/ and came to the pryson with the
frere and the frere sayd to hyr/ Madame we been retorned for
to knowe your good answer/ and your entencyon/ And vyenne
ansuerd/ lordes myn entencyon is that I shal neuer breke my 30
promesse that I haue made/ For I haue auowed that I shal
neuer take husbond/ ne goo oute of this pryson/ but dede sauf
hym to whome I haue promysed/ and therfore retorne ye in

good tyme ¶ Thenne sayd the frere/ by my fayth I wote not
what to say/ for it is grete dommage that ye suffre so moche
sorowe & payne/ and syth it is thus your wylle & that ye wyl
none otherwyse do/ Neuertheles the moure prayeth you/ that
it may playse you to do to hym so moche grace/ that syth ye 5
wyl not take hym in maryage/ that ye wyl were thys rynge
for the loue of hym/ Now thys rynge was the same rynge that
vyenne gaf to parys whan he departed fro hyr in the hows of
the chappelayn/ and vyenne by cause they shold nomore come
ageyn took the rynge/ & whan she had receyued the rynge/ 10
parys sayd to the frere/ I praye you that ye tarye a lytel
wythoute/ For I wyl see what countenaunce she wyl make
of the rynge/ and the frere sayd gladly/ Neuertheles he
meruaylled moche/ and Incontynent the frere wente oute/
and vyenne began to beholde the rynge/ and whan parys 15
sawe that vyenne byhelde the rynge so strongely/ he began
to speke in hys playne tongue/ and sayd/ O moche noble lady
why be ye so moche admeruayled of that rynge/ Thenne sayd
vyenne/ Certes to my semyng I sawe neuer a fayrer/ ¶ Thenne
sayd parys/ Therfore I praye [e iij^v] you that ye take therin 20
playsyr for the more that ye byholde it the more ye shal
prayse it/

Whan Vyenne herde the moure thus speke/ thenne she
was more admeruaylled than tofore/ and was as a
persone al abasshed and sayd/ Alas am I enchaunted/ 25
& what is thys that I see and here speke And in sayeng these
wordes she wold haue fledde for fere oute of the pryson/ by
cause she herde the moure so speke/ thenne sayd parys/ O
moche noble lady vyenne/ meruaylle ye noo thynge/ ne haue
ye noo doubte/ lo here is parys your true seruaunte/ and 30
vyenne was thenne abasshed more than tofore/ Certes sayd
she this may not be but by werke enchaunted/ & parys sayd/
Noble lady hit is none enchaunted werke/ For I am your
seruaunt parys whyche lefte you with ysabeau in suche a
chyrche/ & there ye gaf to me the dyamond whiche now 35
I haue delyuerd to you and there ye promysed to me that ye
wold neuer take husbond but me/ and be ye noo thynge

[*Paris and Vienne*] 75

admeruaylled of the berde ne of the vesture that I were/ for
they take awaye the knowleche of me/ & many other wordes
sayd parys to vyenne/ by whyche she knewe clerely that he
was parys and for the souerayn loue that she bare to hym/ &
for the grete Ioye that she had/ she began to wepe in hys 5
armes/ and tembrace and kysse hym moche swetely/ and
there they comforted eche other wyth swete wordes/ & so
abode longe tyme/ vyenne coude not ynough kysse hym &
enbrace hym/ and also parys demaunded of hyr of hyr aduen-
ture/ & she tolde hym alle/ And of alle thys ysabeau had 10
nothyng herde of/ for she was faste a slepe by cause she had
watched alle the nyght byfore/ and for the grete Ioye and
swetenes that parys & vyenne demeaned bytwene them she
awoke/ and whan she sawe vyenne beyng enbraced with the
moure she sayd/ Madame what is thys that ye do/ haue ye 15
loste your wytte/ that so enbrace this moure/ hath he enchaunted you that ye suffre hym soo famylyer wyth you/ and
is this the fayth that ye kepe to parys/ for whom ye haue
suffred so moche payne & sorowe/ and vyenne sayd/ Swete
suster say ye noo suche wordes/ but come & take your parte 20
of the solace that I haue/ for also wel haue ye founden good
aduenture as I haue/ See ye not here my swete parys/ whome
so moche we haue desyred/ Thenne ysabeau approched ner to
hym & byhelde hym wel and sawe that it was parys/ and she
wente & kyssed hym/ & demened so moche [e iiij^r] grete 25
Ioye bytwene them thre/ that there is noo persone in the
world that myght say ne thynke it/ but so abode a grete
whyle in thys soulas and Ioye/ tyl atte laste parys spack/
Swete vyenne it byhoueth that we goo hens tofore my lord
the dolphyn your fader/ For now fro hens forth it is necessarye 30
that he knowe alle our fayte/ Neuertheles I praye you to say
nothyng/ tyl I desyre you/ and al thre came oute of the
pryson/ and fonde the frere whyche meruaylled gretely and
alle they to gydre wente to the doulphyn/ whyche had
souerayn playsyr whan he saw them And neuertheles he was 35
moche abasshed how his doughter was so come/ and thenne
parys sayd to the frere/ Say ye to the doulphyn that I haue
conuerted hys doughter to hys wylle and to myn/ & that it

playse hym that she be my wyf/ & the frere sayd soo/ Thenne
the doulphyn sayd to hys doughter/ wyl ye take thys man for
your husbond/ whyche hath delyuerd me oute of pryson in
grete peryl of hys persone/ Thenne demaunded vyenne of
Parys yf he wold that she shold speke/ and parys sayd ye/ 5
And thenne Vyenne sayd to the doulphyn/ My fader I am
redy to do your commaundement and hys/ and praye you to
pardonne me & to gyue to me your benedyctyon/ and whan
she sayd thus/ hyr fader pardonned hyr and gaf to hyr hys
blessyng & kyssed hyr/ Thenne sayd vyenne loo here is my 10
good frende Parys whome I haue so moche desyred/ and for
whome I haue suffred so moche payne & sorowe and fader
thys is he that so swetely songe and floyted/ and that wanne
the Ioustes in thys cyte/ and bare with hym the shelde of
crystal and my garlonde/ & also thys is he that wanne the 15
Ioustes in the cyte of paris and wan there the thre baners
wyth the iij Iewellys/ and went awaye with them wythoute
knowyng of ony man/ And also he hath delyuerd you out of
pryson puttyng hys lyf in Ieopardye for you/ and whan the
doulphyn vnderstood al thys he was meruayllously glad and 20
Ioyous/ After al thys parys went to his fader/ & whan he
sawe hym and knewe that he was hys sone parys/ whome he
had so longe desyred to see/ he enbraced hym & kyssed hym/
& for the Ioye that he had he coude not speke a word and
after alle the other lordes & knyghtes ranne for tembrace & 25
kysse hym/ and after this Ioye Parys fader sayd to the
doulphyn/ My lord playse it you that I may borowe my sone
home to my hous for to see his moder and hys felowe Edward
[eiiij^v] ¶Thenne sayd the doulphyn it playseth me ryght wel
onely for thys day/ For to morn I wyl that the maryage of 30
hym & my doughter be made & solempnysed here/ And
thenne messyre Iaques wente with hys sone vnto hys hous/
And whan he was there/ verayly his fader/ his moder/ and
hys felowe Edward wyst not where they were for Ioye and
playsyr that they had and that was noo wonder/ for they had 35
no moo chyldren but hym/ and he shold wedde the doughter
of their lord/ and also Parys was in that tyme become a
valyaunte knyght/ and ful of al beaulte/ and for many reasons

[*Paris and Vienne*] 77

it was no meruayll though they had in hym grete Ioye
and playsyr/ & Edward demaunded of hym of hys aduen-
ture/ & many other thynges/ And he recounted and tolde
hym alle/

¶ *How Parys espoused and wedded vyenne/ and of the feste that
was there made/*

Thenne on the morn the dolphyn gaf his doughter in   5
maryage to parys And the feste was moche noble and
sumptuous/ For moche peple were comen thyder for to
see the feste/ and it endured fyftene dayes/ And the playsyr
and solace whyche was doon for the loue of Parys and of
vyenne was soo grete/ that vnnethe it may be byleued/ whyche 10
parys and Vyenne lyued to gyder a grete whyle in ryght grete
consolacyon and playsyr/ but after thaccomplysshement of
the maryage/ the fader and moder of parys lyueden not longe
after in thys world/ and Parys had by vyenne hys wyf thre
chyldren/ that is to wete two sones & one doughter/ And the 15
doulphyn ordeyned for them moche noble matrymonye/ And
parys after the deth of hys fader and his moder wold that
Edward hys dere felowe shold be herytyer of al the goodes
that hys fader lefte and gaf to hym ysabeau to hys wyf/
whyche lyued to gyder longe tyme in grete loue and con- 20
corde/ And sone after the doulphyn & hys wyf deyeden/ And
thenne was Parys doulphyn[1] and had the possessyon of al the
seygnourye/ the whyche lyued wyth vyenne in thys world
fourty yere and ledde a good and holy lyf/ in so moche that
after thentendement of somme men they be sayntes in heuen/ 25
& they deyed bothe in one yere/ And semblably Edward and
ysabeau deyed bothe tweyne in one yere/ Therfore late vs
praye vnto our lord that we may doo suche werkes in this
world/ that in suche wyse we [e v^r] may accompanye them in
the perdurable glorye of heuen Amen/   30
¶Thus endeth thystorye of the noble and valyaunt knyght
parys/ and the fayr vyenne doughter of the doulphyn of
Vyennoys/ translated out of frensshe in to englysshe by

[1] doulyhyn C.

wylliam Caxton at westmestre fynysshed the last day of August the yere of our lord M CCCC lxxxv/ and enprynted the xix day of decembre the same yere/ and the fyrst yere of the regne of kyng Harry the seuenth/

¶ Explicit p Caxton

NOTES

These notes contain detailed comparison between Caxton's text, the French manuscript, B.N. Fr. 20044, and Gherard Leeu's printed text of 1487. These are referred to respectively as *C*, *MS*, *L*. Minor verbal differences between *MS* and *L* are not noticed. Occasionally comparison is made with the French manuscripts which contain the older and fuller version of the story. They are referred to as *Ver. I*. H denotes Hazlitt's notes to his edition for the Roxburghe Club.

1/1 Same chapter heading in *C*, *L*; no heading in *MS*; *Ver. I* is not divided into chapters. Chapter breaks often occur at different places in *C*, *L*, and *MS* and they often disagree on the text of the headings.

kynge Charles: there was no King Charles of France in 1271. The date may be a late addition to the story since *Ver. I* does not mention one. On the non-historicity of the persons and events in this story see Introd. p. xx.

1/6 **in hauoyr and in landes**: *MS* 'en terre et en tresor'; *L* 'en terre et en auoir'.

1/8 **lordes & barons of his courte**: *MS* 'barons et seigneurs'.

1/10 **& had**: *MS* 'Et celuy dauphin avoit'.

1/11 **lady**: *MS* adds 'la fille du conte de flaundres'.

1/13 þᵗ ... **dyane**: *MS* omits.

1/14 **a lytel**: *MS* omits.

1/15 **replenysshed ... gentylnes**: *MS* 'estoit plaine de toulte noblesse'. **that ... haue**: *MS* omits; *L* 'que dame pourroit ou deburoit auoir'.

1/17 **dyane**: *L* and *MS* add 'sa femme'. **wythoute yssue**: *MS* 'sans filz ne fille'; *L* 'sans auoir enfans'.

1/21 **viij yere of theyr maryage**: *MS* omits; *L* 'sept ans ensemble'.

1/23 **gladnes & Ioye**: *MS*, *L* 'feste'. **daulphyns londe**: *L* 'tout le daulphine'.

1/25 **loue**: *MS* 'noblesse'.

2/3 **bothe**: *MS*, *L* add 'que lune ne pouoit estre sans laultre'.

2/5 **beawte & gentylnesse**: *Ver. I* adds 'et tousjours lysoit livres et romans de belles ystoires. Et daultre part aprenoit a danser et chanter et sonner instrumens de toutes manieres. Et en touz ces faitz estoit gracieuse et plaisant'. This passage is also in the Spanish.

2/5–7 **so that … contrees**: *L* 'et non pas seulement au daulphine mais aussi par toute angleterre et aultres royaulmes fust tenue la plus belle que lon sceust et fut moult loue pour grant dignite de son pere et de sa mere. Si aduint que quand elle fut grande elle fut demandee a femme par moult de roys ducs & aultres grans seigneurs que la desiroient auoir a femme'; *MS* 'Et quant ceste fille fust de lage de xii ans non tant seulement en la terre du dauphine mais en toute france et engleterre fust tenue a grant merueilles la sienne beaulte. Et fut mieulx loue pour la grant dignite de son pere et de sa mere. Et pour la beaulte que estoit en elle demandee estoit por fame de moult grant princes barons et chevaliers de france.'

2/11 **lygnage**: *MS, L* add 'moult puissant de terres de chateaulx et de richesses'. *MS* puts here the clause 'lequel se nommoit, etc.' which *C* and *L* put after 'the whiche was wel byloued'.

2/13 **Iames**: *MS, L* 'Jacques'. **had**: *MS* 'ung notable dame pour feme de laquelle auoit ung moult beau filz', etc.

2/15 **xviij yere**: *MS, L* 'xv ans'; *Ver. I* 'onze ans'.

2/16 **adressed**: *MS, L* add 'et enseigner'.

2/18 **doubed knyght**: *MS* omits; *L* 'et dedens peu de temps fut fait cheualier', etc.

2/28 **lordes**: *MS* 'moult de notables et grans seigneurs et barons et cheualiers'; *L* 'moult daultres grans seigneurs'.

2/30 **bothe of one age**: *Ver. I* adds 'ilz estoient nez tous deux en ung temps et en une saison'.

2/32 **Ioustyng**: *MS* 'qui se faisoient par le monde ou ces deulx cheualiers conqueroient tojours grant fame et grant renomme'; *L* 'et especialement en celles qui se faisoient au royaulme de france/ et si naloient en lieu ou ilz naquissent grant honneur et grant fame'; *MS* and *L* 'et estoient tous deux de tresque et souueraine beaulte en leur ieunesse'.

2/37 **was**: *MS* 'moult gracieulx et estoit'.

3/2–4 **but not … lady**: *MS, L* 'sinon quil auoit enuiron (*MS* seulement) ung an quil auoit commence a aimer la belle Vienne …'

3/5 **that … lord**: *L* omits.

3/13 **parys was amerous of hyr**: *MS* adds 'ne quelle saisoit des aultres cheualiers et barons qui pour lamour delle faisoient tousiours festes et cheualeries'.

3/16 **fyre of loue**: *MS, L* 'lamour'.

3/17 *MS* heading reads 'Comment paris et edouart alerent faire aubades a vienne'; *L* 'Comment paris et edouart faisont les aubades deuant la chambre a vienne'.

Notes

3/18 **melodyous myrthe**: *MS, L* 'aubades'.
3/20 **as recourders**: *MS, L* omit.
3/23 **pypes**: *MS, L* omit.
3/28 **as wel . . . Instrumentes**: *MS* 'chans'; *L* 'chanson'.
3/31 **theyr castel**: *MS, L* omit.
4/3 **they**: *MS, L* 'menestriers'.
4/10 **dysplayseth**: *L* adds 'ma belle & doulce seur'.
4/12 **loue outher you or me**: *MS* 'pour lamour de moy'.
4/13 *L* begins a chapter with the heading: 'Comment le daulphin ordonna dix hommes bien armez pour faire amener deuant luy lesdits menestriers.'
4/15 **that soo sange . . . chambre**: *MS* omits; *L* 'qui venoient faire icelles aubades'.
4/19 **by force or otherwyse**: *MS* 'par gre ou par force'.
4/20 **swete melodye**: *MS, L* 'ce les amenassent deuant luy et de tout cecy fut faict son commandement'. **nyght**: *MS, L* add 'obscure'.
4/22 **thembusshement that was layed**: *MS, L* 'de tout cecy'. **came**: *MS, L, Ver. I, Sp.* add 'auec ung (ieune enfant *L*) enffant qui portoit les instrumens'.
4/25 **playsyr . . . to here**: *MS, L* 'que iamais ne les auoyent faictz telz'.
4/27 **sayeng . . .**: *MS* 'Et un de x hommes leur va dire'.
4/32 **fayr brother**: *MS, L* 'car il convient que nos aduisons de ceste enfant aussi bien comme de nos car sil estoit pris par luy nous serions descouuers'.
5/1 **ye wyl**: *L* adds 'Et adonc paris et edouard firent retourner lenfant a lostel'.
5/6 *L* begins a new chapter: 'Comment Paris & Edouard son compaignon se deffendirent contre dix hommes darmes.'
5/16 *MS* begins a new chapter: 'Comment paris se mist avec levesque de saint laurens.' *Ver. I* 'Saint Vincent'.
5/16 **or not**: *MS, L* add 'mais bien fut grief a iceulx espies de laisser la place et plus que deux mesmes mais pour doubte de mort sen fuirent et par ainsi sans nul dommaige ils eschapperent'.
5/17-19 **daulphyn . . . lyues**: *MS, L* add 'tous naurez et luy conterent le grant dommaige quelz auoient souffert par deux hommes tant seulement et comment a grant vergoigne les auoient conneuuz fuyr et lung estoit naure en la teste laultre aux bras et laultre en la iambe'.
5/26-27 **chargyng . . . vnto hym**: *MS, L* omit.

5/32 **grete lordes**: *MS* 'jeune home de grant vertuz'.
6/1 *MS* begins a new chapter: 'Comment le dauphin fist crier unes jostes.'
6/5 **made lystes . . . sette vp**: *MS*, *L* omit. They add '& ce il faisoit pour donner ioyeusete a vienne sa fille qui de ce fut moult ioyeuse et si en eut moult grant plaisir et dit a ysabeau que par celle feste se pourroit cognoistre qui estoient celux qui tant estoient amoureux delle'.
6/6 **herauldes**: *MS*, *L* omit.
6/7 **in normandye**: *MS*, *L* omit.
6/13 **fyn gold**: *MS*, *L* omit.
6/14 **noble and fayr mayden**: *MS*, *L* omit.
6/16–17 **and she . . . vyenne**: *MS*, *L* omit.
6/19–22 **the moost parte . . . Ioustes**: *MS* and *C* agree; *L* is different: 'des princes et des cheualiers de france dangleterre et de flandres xv ou xvi iours deuant sappareillerent darmes et de cheuaulx pour aller a ces ioustes'.
6/21 **and of Normandye**: *MS*, *L* omit.
6/26 *MS* mentions only four knights, omitting 'wyllyam sone', etc., but after Mountferat *MS* adds 'ces v barons vindrent pour lamour de vienne moult notablement appareilliez lesquielz auoient entendement de faire vaillante cheualiers'; *L* adds this sentence after 'duc de carnes'.
6/31 **fyrst day of May**: *MS*, *L* omit.
7/3 **ij dayes before**: *MS* 'v jours'; *L* 'ung iour'.
7/5 **where as**: *MS* adds 'sa fame et sa fille'.
7/13 **louer**: *MS* 'que estoit delle tant amoureux'; *L* 'estoit enamoure delle'.
7/15 **wete . . . hyr**: *MS*, *L* 'et seruoit moult saigement en regardant la grant beaulte de vienne si que tousiours samour luy croissoit en son cueur touteffois il se gardoit le mieulx quil pouoit que nul ne sen print garde'.
7/16 *MS*, *L* begin a chapter. *MS* 'Coment les joustes se firent'; *L* 'Comment paris gaigna les ioustes en la cite de vienne'.
7/25 **tofore . . . damoyselles**: *MS*, *L* omit.
7/26 *C* is longer and more descriptive. **rydyng . . . Edward**: *MS*, *L* 'par la champ Et tantost la firent et estoyent tous tant noblement abillez que chun disoit icy a beaulx cheualiers & bien armez mais le plus amoureux de tous estoit edouard'.
8/1 **lyon of gold**: *MS* 'lion dazur au champ dargent'; *L* 'lyon dargent'.

Notes

8/10 **speres**: *MS* adds 'et puis mesdrent les mains aux espees et se donnarent de grans coupz merueilleusement'.

8/12 **kept theyr sterops**: *MS, L* omit.

8/15 **Edward the kynges sone of englond**: not mentioned in *Ver. I*, where the fight is with 'ung cheualier' and is technical and detailed.

8/19 **ouerthrewe hym**: *MS* adds 'et sept aultres merueilleux cheualiers'.

8/21 **souper tyme**: *MS, L* 'disner'.

8/27 No break in *MS* but a chapter division in *L*: 'Comment lescu de cristal et le chapelet de fleurs fut donne a paris comme au mieulx faisant.'

8/28 **worshyp & loenge**: *MS, L* 'honneur'.

9/2 *C, MS, L* condense here over *Ver. I* omitting conversation between Paris and Edward and between Vienne and Ysabel.

9/9 Chapter heading in *MS*: 'Ung debat se esleue entre les cheualiers de france et dengleterre.' *Ver. I* by way of parenthetical aside begins here with: 'layrons a parler du dauphin et Vienne ung petit et parlerons dun debat qui naquit en France pour ceste cause'. Then *Ver. I* tells of the rivalry of the three knights over the beauty of Floryane, daughter of Johan de Normandie, Constance, sister of 'ung roy en Angleterre' and of Vienne, daughter of the dauphin. This occupies twenty-two printed lines.

9/16 **bare oute**: *L* 'auoient cognoissance a'.

9/24 **Euer multeplyed . . .**: This sentence is omitted in *MS*: it is replaced by 'Et tosiours la beaute de Vienne multiplioit en grant bruit'.

9/26 **wherof he had grete Ioye**: *MS* begins a chapter here: 'Comment le dauphin et vienne furent courroussiez car ils ne sauoient le cheualiers.'

9/32 **for myn hert gyueth**: *MS, L* 'car le cuer le me dit'. This passage is much longer in *Ver. I* with more details of her love sickness and so also is the passage that follows detailing a similar state in Paris.

10/4 **for tyl now . . .**: *MS, L* 'car jucques ycy ne luy auoit touche au cuer'.

10/6 **nothyng**: *MS* adds 'Et voulentiers laisseroit lamour se il pouvoit'; *L* 'mais leust voulut laisser si luy fust possible honnorablement'. The advice of James (Messire Jacques) is fuller in *Ver. I* and is followed by an equally long reply by Paris (omitted *C, MS, L*) in which Paris affirms his devotion to his parents and asks their pardon for having displeased them.

10/19 **ye took acqueyntaunce:** *MS, L* 'vous acompaignastes (*L* estes acointe auec) dyable deveque'.

10/22 **that hath be holden in vyenne:** *MS, L* omit.

10/30 Chapter heading in *MS*: 'Comment le roy de france va ordonner unes joustes en la cite de paris.' *L* has no chapter heading but a break and then 'On dit icy listorie qui ainsi que ouy auez pour les trois damoiselles deuant dictes quil fut ung grant debat entre les barons dessus dictz.' **Now sayth ... aboue:** *MS* omits.

10/32 **erles:** *MS, L* 'conte'. *Ver. I* reads 'Johan filz du comte de Flandres'.

10/33 **Duc of brennes:** *MS* 'Jehan frere du duc de boheme'; *Ver. I* 'Johan filz du roy de Boheme'. The encounter is much more detailed in *Ver I*. H suggested that Brienne is meant, but pointed out that there were no dukes of Brienne at so early a period. There were, however, counts of Brienne from as early as the thirteenth century. *L* agrees with *C*; *MS, Sp* and *Ver. I* have 'boheme' (i.e. Bohemia).

11/1 **fyue:** *Ver. I* 'pluseurs chevaliers'. **hardy and valyaunte:** *MS* omits; *L* 'vaillans cheualiers'.

11/3 **Florye:** *MS* omits.

11/5 **said & mayntened:** *MS, L* 'disent'.

11/7–9 **mayntened ... world:** *MS, L* 'maintenoyent (et soustenoyent la belle *L*) vienne fille du daulphin'.

11/16 **And whan ... stryf:** *MS, L* omit.

11/19 **viij day of septembre:** *MS, Ver. I* 'la veille de notre dame' (feste *Ver. I*).

11/20–24 **parys ... world:** *MS, L* are more detailed: 'et que ceulx qui seroient meilleurs armes & cheualeries emporteroient lhonneur de ceste feste & que par ce la pucelle qui seroit maintenue par ses cheualiers de france dangleterre & de flandres auroit le pris de laquelle ordonnance les barons furent bien contens'.

11/24 *Ver. I* describes in elaborate detail the furnishings of the field—scaffolds, banners with the names of the fair ladies, etc.

11/31 **stones:** *Ver. I* 'une pierre qui sappelloit charboncle'.

11/37 **tresour:** *MS, L* add 'et lequele luy auoit enuoye la contesse de flandres qui estoit sa dame'.

12/7 **Normandye:** *MS* 'flandres'. *Ver. I* 'de france dangleterre de normandy de flandres'.

12/8 **wytte and entendement:** *MS, L* 'entendement'.

12/11 **bruyt & renomme:** *MS, L* 'bruit'.

12/13 **the quarelle:** *MS, L* omit.

Notes

12/15 **worshyp**: *MS* 'lonneur'; *L* 'ce quilz auoient dit et propose'.

12/19 The extensive motivation for the secrecy is not in *Ver. I*.

13/9–10 **doughter ... vyennoys**: *MS* omits.

13/10 **rede**: *MS, Sp* 'verde'; *L* 'rouge'.

13/12 **whyt**: *MS, L* 'rouge'; *Ver. I* 'vert'; *Sp* 'azul'.

13/17 **ij dayes**: *MS* 'dung jour'; *Sp* 'a quarto de setiembre'; *Ver. I* omits.

13/19 *MS* begins a new chapter: 'Comment le roy de france va ordonner unes joustes en la cite de paris'.

13/21 **xiiij day of septembre**: *MS, Ver. I* omit. *C* introduces new material and changes the order of ideas. *MS* 'Apres que toulx les barons furent venus a paris jamais ne fut veu si grant noblesse en france en engleterre ne en flandres de mains royaulmes et venoient a paris pour veoir ceste feste merueilleuse'. *MS, L* 'Et quant vint au matin le jour des joustes le roy de france fist metre banieres des demoyselles' (*MS* 'iij joyaulx aux troys banieres').

14/1 **hrete** (mistake for **grete**): *MS* 'grant'. Before the account of the king's speech *Ver. I* tells of Paris and Edward coming to Paris in disguise and taking their places under the banner of Vienne.

14/7 **loue and of curtosye**: *MS* 'lonneur de celle cheualerie'.

14/10 **the prys and thonour**: *MS* 'pris de la beaute'.

14/22 **of Normandye**: *MS* 'de fleurine de normendie'.

14/23 **Vyenne**: *MS* adds 'sur cheuaulx bien abilles'.

14/24 **Normandye**: *MS* 'florine'.

14/25 **therle**: *MS, L* 'conte'.

14/26 **Phelyp**: *MS* 'Felix'. The list of knights varies considerably in the various texts. *C, L, MS* agree closely. Several of the names and the order are different in *Ver. I*; the Spanish is again different.

14/27 **erle of Armynak**: *MS* 'conte de la marche'; *L* 'conte darmaignat'.

14/31 **sone of the duc of bremeos**: *MS* 'frere du roy de bohemie'; *L* 'filz du duc de breuues'.

14/33 **the honourable Iohan of braban**: *MS* omits.

14/34 **therle**: *MS, L* 'conte'.

14/36 **baner**: *L* 'maniere'. **fayr vyenne**: *MS* 'ma dame de vienne'.

15/2 **Antonye ... prouynce**: *MS* omits.

15/6 **wel horsed**: *MS* omits; *L* 'bien montez'.

15/10 **armed**: *MS* 'armez et abillez'.

15/11 No heading or chapter break in *MS*; *L* 'Comment paris gaigna ioustes en la cite de paris.'

15/12 **hour of tyerce**: not in *Ver. I*.

15/15 **sone of the duke of brennes**: *MS* 'frere du roy bohemie'.

15/18 **Edward**: *MS* 'orugo'.

15/19 **ij knyghtes**: *MS* 'ces troyes cheualiers'. This passage is much confused in *MS*. The order is: John of Flanders, John of Bohemia, Orugo of Bourbon, Edward of Burgoyne, John peryllous, Anthony Allegret, Paris.

15/23 **day or nyght**: *MS* 'vif ou mort'.

15/28–30 **After . . . erthe**: *MS* omits. There is no mention of Geoffrey here in *MS* but in the next sentence Paris is fighting against Geoffrey.

15/34 **they gaf . . . therthe**: the details of the tournament are different in *Ver. I* and the account is much expanded: 'Et le chevalier vint pareillement de lautre couste si sentredonnerent de si grans cops que les lances rompirent si que les pieces en vouloient par laer Les coups furent grans et pesans et les chevaulx ne les peurent sostenir si versarent lun desa laultre dela le dos vers la terre et les pies contre le ciel.'

16/4 **& came rennyng**: *MS* omits.

16/5 **hors slode**: not in *Ver. I*; there Paris throws horse and rider 'tout en ung mont', but the rider without losing the reins mounts again.

16/20 Paris's speech in *Ver. I* is twenty printed lines long but its content is the same as here.

16/24 **another tyme**: *MS* adds 'ou deulx ou troyes'.

16/33 It is a longer and more equal fight in *Ver. I*.

17/1 **normandye**: *MS* 'florine'.

17/2 In *MS* 'pierre filz du duc de normendie' is placed after 'Balexo', and 'phelyp of bauyere' (17/3) does not appear. *Ver. I* omits the names.

17/6 **brother . . . marche**: *MS* omits.

17/8 **and whan parys saw . . .**: *MS* is more detailed and clearer: 'Et paris va respondre que non obstant quil fust toult seul auant quil faillisent du champ quil voulloit venir a la fin.'

17/9 **he fewtred hys spere**: *MS* 'Et brocha son cheual et va vers eulx'; *L* 'baissa sa lance et vint vers eulx'.

17/12 **vnder hys hors**: *MS* omits.

17/14 No chapter break in *MS*; *L* 'Commentl e roy fist donner les trois banieres auec les trois ioiaulx a paris champion de vienne'.

Notes 87

17/17 **kynge**: *MS* adds 'of france' and omits **& the other ... knyghtes.**

17/25 *Ver. I* at this point is much longer with an account of the awarding of the prizes, the proclamation of Vienne as the most beautiful girl, and the departure of Paris and Edward secretly to a village ten leagues away.

17/29 **thonour of the Ioustes**: *MS* 'loneur du dauphin qui retourna de paris a vienne avec messire jacques'. *MS* here is inconsistent with 18/14.

17/30 *Ver. I* tells of Paris placing his prizes around the altar in his 'petite garde roube'.

18/15 In *Ver. I* the homecoming is elaborately described with an account of the assembly of all the Dauphin's men, and a long address to them by the Dauphin telling them that an unknown knight had fought to prove Vienne the most beautiful, had vanquished twenty-two knights, including Godeffroy of Picardye, and that he had brought back the prize for Vienne, a crown of gold.

18/35 **I praye ... honour**: *MS* 'je prie a dieu tout puissant quil luy doint bien et honneur'.

19/20 **wepe & waylle**: *MS* 'plourer et souspirer'.

19/21 **but none ... ysabeau**: *MS* omits but adds 'et ainsy daultre part paris passoit son temps en douloureuse vie le plus secretment quil pouoit'.

19/22 *MS* begins a new chapter: 'Comment missere jacques disoit a paris pourquoy nestoit alle a la cite de paris.'

19/30 **heuynesse**: *MS* omits; *L* 'tristesse'.

19/32 **thys bysshop**: *MS* 'ce dyable devecque'.

19/36 **amytye**: *MS* omits. This speech of Paris's father is forty-three printed lines long in *Ver. I*.

20/6 **whyche am soo meschaunt**: *MS* omits.

20/24 **honnest**: *MS* omits.

20/30 **my lady**: *Ver. I* calls her 'madame de Berbant'.

20/36 **closed them fast in his chambre**: *MS* omits.

21/3 **worshyp**: *L, MS* omit. **were moche praysed**: *MS* 'il gaignerent honneur grant et lamour des dames et damoiselles et des cheualiers'.

21/7 Chapter heading in *MS*: 'Comment vienne prist le banere en loritoire de paris'; in *L*: 'Comment dyane et vienne allerent visiter le pere de paris lequel estoit malade.'

21/10 **or accesse**: *MS, L* omit; *Ver. I* 'fivre continue'.

21/18 **and ysabeau ... companye**: *MS* omits.

21/21 **and laye**: *MS* omits.
21/25 **bysshop**: *MS* 'dyable devesque'.
21/27 **wyth the goodes . . . to me**: *MS* omits.
21/33 **castel**: *MS* adds 'lequel estoit moult beau aloient regarder'. This is a delightful passage in *Ver. I*, for it is a detailed description of the circuit of the castle.
22/4–5 **After she ladde . . . fowles of chace**: *MS* omits; *L* 'ou il y auoit faulcons octours et maintz aultres oyseaulx de chasse'.
22/14 **fayr syster**: *MS* omits.
22/15 **Parys**: *MS* omits.
22/21 **& the garlond**: *MS* omits.
22/26–28 **Madame . . . chambre**: *MS*, *L* 'ma dame grant mal mest venu (*MS* sur le cuer) pourquoy sil vous plaisoit je me vouldroye ung petit poser (*L* peu reposer) en ceste chambre'.
22/30 **shytte**: *L* 'ferma la porte de la chambre par derriere'.
22/31 **that none myght come in**: *MS*, *L* omit. **vyenne**: *L* adds 'a ysabeau'.
22/32 **that . . . knowleche of**: *MS* 'que nous en trouverons encore'. At this point *MS* begins a new chapter: 'Comment vienne faisoit ses plains a ysabel.'
23/1 **whyche was xij foot longe**: *MS*, *L* omit; *Sp* agrees with *C*.
23/2 **mageste**: *MS* 'limage'.
23/6 **thre baners . . . Parys**: *MS* 'la baniere blanche au bout toute desployee que le cristil paris avoit gaignee en la cite de paris'.
23/8 **And in the same place**: *MS* omits.
23/15 **she sette . . .**: *Ver. I* 'Et lors elle se mist a genoilx davant lotel et commenca a cryer a haulte voix Paris Paris Paris.' Then follow seven lines of apostrophe and exclamation ending 'si se gicta davant lotel et la commenca a plorer molt tendrement et gicter grant habundance de larmes'. **on the grounde**: *MS* omits.
23/16 **word**: *MS*, *L* add 'Et quand elle fut reposee si dit (*MS* fut sappaisee va dire)'.
23/20 **who he was that . . .**: *MS* omits.
23/22 **to repreue**: *MS* 'adviser et reprendre'.
23/24 **folye**: *MS* adds 'et dueil'; *L* adds 'et vueillez user de vostre bon sens'. **wysedom and reason**: *MS* 'bon sens'.
23/31 **on ysabeau**: *MS* omits.
23/32 **veray**: *MS*, *L* omit.
24/5 **custommes**: *MS* omits.
24/9 **lordes**: *MS* adds 'of France'.
24/21 **me**: There follows a long passage in *L* which is not in *C*,

MS: 'Et pource ne soyes pas esbahie/ se iay mis mon amour a luy/ car le cas pareil est aduenu a plusieurs aultres nobles dames et damoiselles/ Comme nos lisons de la fille du noble roy darmenie nommee iusiana/ qui sestoit enamouree de son chambellan/ sans riens sauoir de son lignaige ou extraction/ Mais pour lamour de ce quil auoit plusieurs fois aeunture son corps et mis en peril tant par mer comme par terre pour lamour de son pere et delle pourquoy ne desiroit aultre mary ne empereur ne roy/que iceluy chambellan Car elle sapercheuoit bien par ses vaillans fais darmes/ quil debuoit estre de noble et vertueuse generation. & fit tant par plusieurs subtilitez et temptations quelle sceut son nom/ le qui estoit bauduyn dauston/fils du conte dauston. Et adoncques quand ysabeau eut ouy ces parolles de sa seur vienne/ il luy sembla en son couraige/ que plus ne luy despriseroit damer le noble et vaillant paris. de paour que ladicte vienne nen print grant desplaisir. & en peut venir a desespararion. et den abregier sa vie, comme elle lui auoit dit. dont elle doubtoit estre cause de sa mort. Comme aultre fois estoit aduenu a plusieurs persones tant hommes comme femes/ lesquelz estoient si fort enamourez lung de laultre dont nesperoient point de confort pour ce que luy estoient trop nobles ou non pareilz de generation ou dauoir. dont vindrent en tel desespoir quil en morurent.'

24/21 **And thus ... stynte :** *L* omits.

24/24 **Vyenne ... lady :** *MS* 'comment estoit a vienne'. **And ysabeau ... anone :** *MS* 'Et ysabel va dire que bien'; *L* 'tantost saillit dehors'.

24/25-26 **And vyenne ... ysabeau :** *MS* omits this sentence.

24/31 **and other Iewellys :** *MS*, *L* omit.

24/32 **Iaques :** *MS* adds 'et de sa fame'. *Ver. I* expands with a scene between Vienne and Ysabel. They look at the banners and jewels and Vienne laments that Paris is not there. That night she dreams of him.

25/1-17 These seventeen lines are not in *Ver. I*. It says simply: 'Lendemain Paris et Edoardo revenyrent de Brebant.' Same heading in *C* and *L*; *MS* adds: 'et retournerent a vienne'.

25/3 **loue of hyr :** *MS* omits.

25/4 **felowe :** *MS* adds 'odouart'.

25/6 **space of v dayes :** *MS* 'aucuns jours'.

25/8 **pleseth it you to wete :** *MS* 'jay receu lettres de mon pere qui est fort mallade'.

25/11 **yf it playse god :** *MS* omits.

90 *Notes*

25/12 **and hys good wylle**: *MS* omits.
25/13 **content & plesyd**: *MS* 'bien luy plaisoit'.
25/20 **and prayers**: *MS*, *L* omit. In *Ver. I* the account of the call on the Dauphin comes here; it is detailed, telling among other things of the new robe which Paris brought from Brabant, exactly like the one Vienne had seen in her dream.
25/26 **and shytte**: *MS*, *L* omit.
25/28 In *Ver. I* Paris's mother has forgotten about the visit of Vienne and her mother; so Paris thinks that thieves have stolen his things.
26/5 **and cladde**: *MS* omits.
26/9 **demaunded hym ... thynges**: *MS* 'va demander nouvelles de maintes choses'.
26/14 **contente ne fylled**: *MS* 'pouvoyt faillier de regarder'; *L* 'saouler de regarder'.
26/15 **and frende**: *MS* omits.
26/23 New chapter in *MS*: 'Comment vienne se confessa a leuesque de saint lorens.' *Ver. I* adds a scene here. Paris goes to the castle of the Dauphin. Vienne sees him from the window. There follows a delightful, playful conversation between Vienne and Ysabel and then comes the plan to call on the services of the bishop.
26/25 **ysabeau**: *MS* adds 'helas'.
26/27 **pensyf**: *MS* adds 'en son courage'.
26/31 **and secretely**: *MS* omits.
26/32 *Ver. I* contains here a long conversation between Vienne and her mother.
27/1 **good wylle**: *MS* adds 'et bonne conscience'.
27/15 No break in *MS*, but *C* and *L* agree: 'Comment la belle Vienne descouurit son couraige a paris.' The scene in *Ver. II* is a short synopsis of the extended scene in *Ver. I*.
27/17 **parys**[2]: *MS* adds 'moult courtoysement'.
27/23 **whyche thenne was seek**: *MS* omits.
27/25 **Iewellys**: *MS* 'choses'.
27/28 **maad ony defaulte**: *MS* omits.
27/30 **none euyl**: *MS* 'vostre mal'.
27/30–31 **humbly and wyth grete reuerence**: *MS* 'a humble reuerence'.
28/3 **Iewellys**: *MS* 'choses'; so also at 28/6. **I ensure you**: *MS* omits.
28/10 **seruyce**: *MS* 'commandement'.
28/11 **frensshe**: *MS* omits.

Notes 91

28/14 **Iewels**: MS 'besoignes'. **as wel as ye**: MS omits.
28/30 **xviij**: MS, L 'viij'. But note that C, L say at 13/21, 'xiiij'; MS 'viij'.
29/17 **caas**: MS 'amours'.
29/21 **spoken**: MS omits.
29/24 **be submysed**: MS 'sunt subgez'; L 'submis'.
29/25 **Parys**: L adds 'moult honourablement'.
30/10 There is no such scene in *Ver. I*, but a similar one between Vienne and Ysabel.
30/11 **and frende**: MS omits.
30/12 **Iape ne truffes**: MS 'nye chose de truffes'; L 'na point truffe'.
30/17 **the fayre vyenne**: MS 'sa dame vienne'. MS begins a new chapter: 'Comment vienne disoit a paris quil seroit son mari.'
30/19 **xv**: *Ver. I* omits.
30/20 **prynces**: MS 'barons'.
30/22 **in treatyng ... ennoyed**: MS 'Paris sentit aucunes choses de quoy fust moult courroucie'.
30/27 C and MS omit a sentence in L: 'O doulce Vienne que veult a dire que ma force & mon aduenture est si tost habaudonnee.'
31/3 **ordure**: MS 'deshonneur'.
31/10-11 **and that ... deffaute**: MS omits.
31/11 **& desyre**: MS omits.
31/16 **entendement**: MS 'hardiment'.
31/19 **hondred thousand**: MS 'dousse mille'.
31/23 **and honourable**: MS omits.
31/27 **for the**: MS 'pour lamour de vous'. **by ... of god**: MS, L omit.
31/29 **and promesse**: MS omits.
31/32 **& requyre**: MS omits.
32/1 **doughter**: MS, L 'folie'. Caxton has evidently misread 'fille' for 'folie'.
32/6 **that I am half confused**: MS adds 'que je meurs'.
32/7 rather than 32/10 begins a new chapter in L, MS: L 'Comment messire iacques demanda au daulphin sa fille Vienne par mariage pour son filz paris'; MS 'Comment missire jacques requist la fille du dauphin'. **that he do it not**: this is a literal translation; **he** refers to the Dauphin and **it** to the Dauphin's consent to the marriage. MS 'Et suis aussi contente quil ne se fasst pas comme que il se faisoit.'
32/32 **hous**: MS 'filz'.

33/3 **in grete thouȝt**: *MS* omits. Before the Dauphin's interview with his daughter, Vienne discusses the matter with Edward (Paris in *Sp*.).
33/7 **& made ... hym**: *MS* omits.
33/11–12 **I wold ... menchon**: *MS* 'vous seroye mourir ou vous tendroye en prison'. *L* omits 'menchon'. *Ver. I* contains no suggestion of making her a nun.
33/13 **contente**: *MS* 'bien joyeuse et contente'.
33/15 In *Ver. I* Vienne after the interview with her father has a long conversation on the subject with Ysabel. Then follows a scene between Paris and Edward on the same subject.
33/16–17 **ayenst ... sone**: *MS* omits.
33/24 **and angre**: *MS* omits.
34/1 This scene is not in *Ver. I*. *L* begins a new chapter: 'Comment Paris parla a Vienne par la fenestre.'
34/4 **hurte**: *MS* 'tuer'.
34/9 **euyll**: *MS* omits.
34/12 **your**: *MS* 'me'.
34/13 **what someuer come therof**: *MS* 'deuesse mourir'.
34/18 **may**: *MS* adds 'et le plus secretement'.
34/21 **lordshyppe**: *MS* 'terre'. **may lyue ... surely**: *MS* 'en maniere que nous nayons paour de rien'.
34/24 **ye touche ... body**: not in *Ver. I*.
34/32 **man**: *MS* 'amy'.
34/33 **george**: *Ver. I* 'Oliver'.
35/3 **rancour**: *MS* omits. In *Ver. I* Paris tells Oliver that a friend of his who has displeased the Dauphin must flee the country.
35/15 **Incontynent**: *MS* omits. In *Ver. I* Oliver's activity at Aygues Mortes is described in detail. He hires an armed 'galee de Genevoys', etc.
35/16 **establisshed**: *MS* 'establit en toulx les passaiges cheuaux'.
35/18 **& came ageyn**: *MS* 'et sen alla en la cite de vienne'.
35/19 **Ioyous**: *MS* adds 'Et le pria quil sen allast auec luy Et luy promist que ainsy seroit.'
35/24 **two hors**: *L* 'bons cheuaulx'. This is all more detailed in *MS*: 'il (Paris) dist a George quil allast a lostel son pere et que luy auec varlet prinssent deulx cheuaux et que gardast bien que son pere ne sen aduisast et que apres sen allases hors de la cite et que lattendissent en ung certain lieu jusques il feussent venus'.
35/26–29 **& Edward ... it**: *MS* puts this sentence after **redy** l. 23. Not in *Ver. I*.

35/30 Heading in *MS*: 'de paris qui sen alloit'; in *L*: 'Comment paris emmena vienne & ysabeau furtiuement de nuyct'.
35/32 **the secretest wyse**: *MS*, *L* omit.
35/33 **houre taken**: *MS*, *L* 'a heure du premier somme'.
35/34 **cladde ... lepen**: *MS* 'sortirent comme hommes et saillirent'.
36/6 **by cause ... waye**: *MS* 'pour monstrer le chemin'.
36/8 **endured ... nyght**: *MS*, *L* 'dura jusques a lendemain a vespres'.
36/9 **towne**: *MS* 'vallee'. In *Ver. I* in searching for a hostel they meet the priest who tells them that there is no inn; whereupon Paris prevails on him to take them in.
36/11 **fonde**: *MS* adds 'moult volentiers'.
36/12 **gladly ... myght**: *MS* 'en ung petit hostel qui estoit loingnant de leglise'.
36/15 **parys seruaunte**: *MS*, *L* 'varlet'.
36/27 **abasshed**: *MS* 'courroucie'.
36/27-34 Not in *Ver. I*.
36/29 **And after ... bycomen**: *MS* omits.
36/34 **and fere**: *MS*, *L* omit.
37/4 **ony men ... brydge**: *MS* 'nul maistre fustier que par nul engin peust faire pont'; *L* 'aulcuns fustiers qui voulissent faire ung pont'.
37/11 *MS*, *L* begin a new chapter. *MS* 'du dauphin qui faisoit sercher vienne par (*word illeg.*) ses terres'; *L* 'Comment le daulphin fit cercher vienne par ses seruiteurs.'
37/14 **troubled**: *MS* adds 'nestoit pas sans cause'.
37/18 **Vyenne**: *MS* 'paris et vienne'.
37/20 **foteman**: *MS* 'cest homme'. *MS* adds a sentence: 'Et lors luy demanda le chapelain sil avoit gens qui se estoyent (*illeg. word*).'
37/23 Portions of f. 28ʳ and f. 28ᵛ are missing in *MS*.
38/6 **men**: *L* 'hommes darmes a cheual'.
38/8 **heuy and melancolyous**: *MS* 'courroucie'.
38/37 **took to hyr hert**: *MS* 'print cuer en soy'.
39/4 **and so ... owne**: *MS* omits.
39/8 **haue trybulacyons**: *MS* 'souffir paine et tribulacion'.
39/11 **comforte**: *MS* has 'conseille' in both places.
39/12 **and frende**: *MS* omits.
39/22 **hope**: *MS* adds 'en dieu'.
39/30 No new chapter in *MS*. *C* and *L* agree on heading.

39/31 **kyssed**: MS 'va baissier et embrasser'.
39/33 **Ihesu Cryste**: MS omits.
40/3 *Ver. I* tells of his going alone so overcome with grief that he falls from his horse and is rescued by two merchants.
40/5 **and as despayred**: MS 'Et quasi demy despare.'
40/6 **water ... aualed**: MS omits.
40/10 **and rowed**: MS omits.
40/13 **fool**: accidentally omitted in MS. **pensyf**: MS 'en pencement et ymaginacion'.
40/17 **whyche ... hous**: MS omits.
40/18 Heading in MS: 'Comment vienne se retourna a la merci de son pere'; in *L*: 'Comment vienne fut ramenee a lotel de son pere'.
40/23 **and that it was force**: MS 'Et vit quelle luy estoit force de retourner'.
40/24 **she appeased hyr self**: MS omits. MS adds '(Vienne) dist au chappelain quil fist venir cel homme a pie quil auoit trouue en la ville'.
40/33 **founden hyr**: MS adds 'en hostel du chappelain'.
41/7 **shall see you**: MS adds 'car il vous cuyde avoir perdue'. **that he shal pardonne**: MS omits.
41/13 MS, L begin chapter: MS 'Comment Vienne demanda pardon a son pere'; L 'Comment Vienne fut ramenee a lostel de son pere'. In *Ver. I* the Dauphin takes the priest aside and questions him before he talks to his daughter. **Now sayth thystory that**: MS omits.
41/14 **heuy**: MS omits.
41/18 **mesprysed**: MS omits.
41/19 **desplaysyr**: MS 'confusion et vergoigne'.
41/21 **Royame of fraunce**: MS 'du monde'.
41/21–23 **allewaye ... pareylle**: MS omits.
41/26 **mercy**: MS 'pouoir et puissance'.
41/28 **by my soule**: MS, L add 'en dieu'.
41/31 **trouthe**: MS adds 'et adonc le dauphin tira le chapelain apart et linterroga'.
41/34 C, MS, L all contain the chaplain's statement that he believed the 'fayre knyght' was drowned while passing a river. Where this comes from is hard to determine. *Ver. I* contains it too. It is inconsistent with what precedes and with what follows, and certainly the Dauphin does not react as if he thought that Paris was dead. **And they were ... wyth me**: MS 'mais les

Notes

deulx damoyselles dormirent ensemble Et les cheualiers et moy dormires en ung lit'.
41/36 **two slepte in the stable**: *MS* omits.
42/3 **& grete yeftes**: *MS* omits.
42/5 **by the hande ... gretely**: *MS* omits.
42/8 **two**: *MS* adds 'moult aigrement et en especial ysabel laquelle se excusoit le mieulx quelle pouoyt disant ...'
42/9 **pure**: *MS* omits.
42/10 **that she departed**: *MS* 'quelle nasquit'.
42/16 **vyenne**: *MS* adds 'toute triste'.
42/21 **and thretene**: *MS* omits.
42/22 **shortly gyue ...**: literally so in *MS, L*.
42/28 At this point *Ver. I* contains a scene in Vienne's mother's bedroom; present are Vienne, her mother, father, and Isabel.
42/33 **and thretened**: *MS* omits.
42/34 **contynuelly ... Parys**: *MS* 'toult le pensement de Vienne estoit continuellement a Paris'.
43/2 **alle ... Parys**: *MS* omits; *L* 'tousiours desirant paris'.
43/4 *MS* begins a new chapter: 'Comment le dauphin fist mestre sa fille hors de prison.'
43/11 **certayn tyme**: *MS* 'ung petit de temps'; *L* 'aulcuns iours'.
43/12 **Erle**: *MS, L* 'conte'.
43/14 **For ... chargeable**: *MS, L* 'car il len chargoit'.
43/16–17 **but euer ... parys**: *MS* 'car toult son entendement estoit en son doulz amy paris'.
43/18 **and knewe ... lyue**: *MS* omits.
44/8 **tyme ... myght**: *MS* 'a grant doleur'.
44/10 *MS, L* begin a new chapter: *MS* 'Comment le conte de Flandres manda au dauphin une lettre'; no heading in *L. Ver. I* inserts a detailed account of Paris's life in Genes.
44/10 **Erle**: *MS, L* 'conte'. This episode occurs later in *Ver. I*.
44/12 **xv**: *Ver. I* 'xiiij'.
44/14 **sone**: *Ver. I* 'nepveu'.
44/36 **as for hys partye**: a literal translation. *MS* adds 'Et le hastoit tant comme il pouvoyt mais encores le hastoit plus le fils du duc de bourgoigne.'
45/1 Chapter division in *MS* and *L* comes after the next line. *MS* 'Comment paris va commander une lettre a son pere & a son compaignon odouart'; *L* 'Comment paris manda de ses nouuelles a edouard son compaignon'.

Notes

45/6 **abode ... allone:** *MS*, *L* 'et demouroit en ung hotel (*L* chasteau) tout seul auec son varlet'.

45/16 *MS* adds 'lettre que paris enuoye a son pere'.

45/17 Compare the letter in *C* with that in *Ver. I*: 'Mon tres honoure seigneur et pere, je recommande a vous si tres humblement comme je puis. Et vous plaise ascavoir que je suis en tres grant soussy et malencolye que je ne puis scavoir novelles de vous et ne scay, se pour adventure le dauphin vous ha fait aucun ennuy ou dommaige, dont je me dobte grandement pour cause de la requeste que vous luy fistes pour moy. Et portant vous supply que il vous plaise moy rescripre, se il vous est possible. Et vous plaise pour Dieu moy pardonner tout ce que je mesfeis oncques vers vous, affin que, quant a Dieu plaire que je doye finer ma doleureuse vie, que je meure en vostre grace, affin que Dieu ait mercy de mon ame.'

45/19 **aduenture ... sorowe:** *MS* omits.

45/20 **payne and trybulacyon:** *MS* 'mal et desplaiser'.

45/23 *MS* is somewhat different: 'Car tout ma vie est de aymer et penser que dicy en avant vous ne me verres plus car je men vueil partir dicy et aller chercher le boult du monde par pellerignages.'

45/32 **and that he ... me:** *MS* omits but adds 'et ceste la derniere chose et grace que je vous pense a requierir et demander'.

45/34 **holy ghoost ... you:** *MS* 'saint esperit soit garde de vous'. **Recomaunde ... &c:** *MS* omits.

45/35 **thus:** *MS* 'en ceste maniere lettre enuoyee a odouart par Paris son compaignon'. In *Ver. I* Paris's father shares the letter with Edward who tells Vienne about it. She asks Edward to write to Paris. He does so, telling Paris all the news of Vienne and his father and telling him to go to the bank of Messire Bertrand de Picartville if he needs money. Then follows the account of Paris's receiving the letter, his drawing the money, renting a chamber in the city, and hiring a valet. Much time he spent in church but constantly he thought of Vienne.

46/2 **peryl of:** *MS* 'le pouvre', *L* 'peril'. **is poursyewed:** *MS* 'vous salue'. Here follows in *Ver. I* the long account of the attempt to make Vienne marry the son of the Duke of Burgundy. There is no mention of a letter to Edward, Edward's visit to Vienne, Edward's reply, Paris's reception of the letter.

46/21 **for thabsence ... persone:** *MS* omits.

47/1 **late ... house:** *MS*, *Ver. I* make better sense than *C*, *L*. *MS* 'mit la lettre a lostel de messere octe de plaisance a geyne'; *Ver. I* 'Jacques de Plaisance'.

Notes

47/2   *MS* begins a chapter: 'Comment odouard monstra la lettra de paris a vienne'.
47/9   **herde**: *MS* 'acheve de lire'.
47/11 **thys letter**: *MS* 'bonnes nouuelles' and adds 'pourquoy soyes joyeulz et veez vous cy une lettre'.
47/32 **wyth myn honour**: *MS* omits.
47/36 **god**: *MS* 'luy', i.e. Paris.
48/1   **vysage**: *MS* omits.
48/9   Caxton condenses with the result that Edward seems to be saying 'for assone shal I gyue . . . wel' 48/10–12. *MS* puts it clearly. **yes sayd she . . . wyl wel**: *MS* 'Il est verite dist vienne Mais ne me parlez plus de la lettre car aussitost vous donnoige ma vie mais si vous voulles aultre chose demandes le moy.'
48/15 Chapter heading in *MS*: 'Comment la lettre que odouart estap (?) a paris estant en la cite de geyne'; in *L* 'Comment edouard manda la response a paris en la cite de gens'.
48/21 **alle hys euyl wylle**: *MS* omits.
48/26 **For al hyr consolacyon . . . you**: *MS* 'car jamais ne pouvoit avoir consolacion jousques a ce quelle a eu nouuelles de vous' is clearer.
48/29 **fro hyr**: *MS* omits.
48/31 **floryns**: *MS* 'frans'; *Sp* 'seys mil ducados'. *Ver. I* is interesting here: 'et si vous aves riens besoing, alles au banc de messire Bertrand de Picartville quar nous luy avons mande quil vous fasse deliverer mille escus'.
49/1   **thanked be god**: *MS* omits.
49/2–4 **letter/whyche . . . said letter**: *C, L* are more detailed than *MS*.
49/5   **the doulphyn . . . duc**: *MS* 'le daulphin luy parle de mari et luy veult donner le fils du duc'; *L* 'luy a traicte mary lequel est filz du duc'.
49/6   **& he hopeth . . . accomplysshed**: *MS* omits and adds 'mais elle ne le veult consentir et nescet quelle fera'.
49/13 **& protectyon**: *MS* omits. **whan thys letter . . . abode**: *MS* omits.
49/17 *MS* begins chapter: 'Comment paris receust le change de iij mille florins'. Note 'frans' above.
49/17 **noble**: *MS* omits.
49/20 **& moche . . . hym self**: *MS* omits.
49/22 **suffre**: *MS* adds 'ne que dyable vous a conseille'.
50/1–3 **And euery moneth . . . reherce**: *MS* omits.

50/3 **& torne ... vyenne :** MS 'Et laissons paris et retournerons au conte de flandres.'
50/5 MS, L begin chapter: MS 'Comment le fils du duc de Burgoigne alla la cite de vienne'. L 'Comment le filz du duc de bourgoigne auec belle compaignie vint au daulphine pour veoir vienne son espeuse/ et pour lemmener auec luy. & comment il fut receu en grand ioye du daulphin/ pere de ladicte vienne.'
50/14 **horses and peple :** MS 'de vestemens et de joyaulx et de chevaulx et de maintes riches choses'.
50/16 **therle :** MS 'conte'.
50/17 **two dayes :** MS omits.
50/30 **affectyon :** MS 'esperance'.
51/5–6 **playsyr ... agreable :** MS 'au nom de nostre seigneur'.
51/6 **Thenne vyenne :** this is preceded in MS by 'Et quant viene eust ouy ses parolles dist.'
51/14 **euyl dysposed :** not in MS. In Ver. I she says she 'veult a Dieu garder son pucellage'.
51/15–16 **causeth me ... maryed.** MS puts it differently: 'Et auec le mal que jay maintenant nul ne pouuroit auoir plaisir de moy.' And then MS adds 'Pourque vous prie en honneur de jesu crist que pour le present ne me forcez de mariage.'
51/19 **he :** MS 'le pere et la mere'.
51/20 **euery day :** MS 'toulte la nuyt'.
51/22 **wylle :** MS 'courage et la voulente'.
51/25 **wherof :** MS 'de la quelle venu'. **playsyr :** MS omits and adds 'et la feste fust apareillee moult noblement a merueiller'.
51/27 **daunce/ synge/ ... playsyrs :** MS 'se donner plaisir en joye en diuerses manieres'.
51/35–52/1 **And thenne ... lyghtly :** MS 'Et le filz du duc de bourgoigne qui estoit de bonne condicion le croit.'
52/4 **consente :** MS adds 'au mariage et quil ne venissent a si grant vergoigne et confusion Et voyant le dauphin que par menasses ne par prieres ne pouoit riens achever commanda ...'
52/5 **vyenne ... manere :** MS 'demoura vienne ainsy bien quinze jours'.
52/8 **& payne :** MS omits.
52/21 **effecte :** MS adds 'car je voy que sa maladie sera longue et plus que ne semble dequoy jay tres grant desplaisir non tant seullement pour elle mais encore pour lamour de vous Et si vous promez que aussi tost quelle sera guerie je le vous manderay'.

52/25 **retorned ... helthe:** MS 'retourna et compta a son pere que vienne nestoit pas saine'.

52/28 Chapter heading in MS: 'Comment le daulphin fist mettre sa fille vienne en prison'; L 'Comment le daulphin fist emprisonner vienne pource quelle ne vouloit consentir au mariage au filz du duc de bourgoigne'.

52/32 **Iayler:** Ver. I 'quatre maistres massons'. They built an underground prison.

53/6–18 Not in Ver. I.

53/9 **and wyth swete wordes:** MS 'Et par grant couraige et doulces parolles ...'

53/16 **vysage:** MS 'amour'.

53/19 Chapter heading in MS: 'Comment vienne mist deulx quartiers de poule soubz ses deulx esselles.' **longe tyme:** MS 'petit de temps'. Ver. I here speaks of Paris who has heard rumours that Vienne is married to the son of the Duke of Burgundy. He writes to Edward but not the same letter as in C 46/1, but rather like C 58/10, asking news of Vienne. Ver. I shows a different order of incidents. 'Le vraye hystoire nous racompte', the author tells us (as if he is perfectly aware of the two versions), that Edward went to the castle to find out news of Vienne, and learned of the house the masons had built and of its location by getting the masons drunk. The next day he went to the priory and told the prior that he would build a chapel. He selected a site over Vienne's subterranean prison and so was able, by knocking out a stone, to speak to her and show her Paris's letter. Then follows the incident as in C 53/19.

53/21 **& that was for ... beaute of hyr:** MS omits.

53/23 **and so concluded ... hyr:** MS 'Et au plus secretement quil peust il sen alla au dauphine pour veoir vienne et pour sauoir comment elle estoit.'

53/25 **gladly and with grete honour:** MS 'a grant joye'.

53/27 **also seke as she was:** C carries over the French idiom: 'ainsy malade comme elle estoit'.

53/29 **& desyre:** MS omits and adds 'quil ne luy pouoyt plus celler va dire'.

54/3 **derke and:** MS omits.

54/14 **Thenne he sente ... hyr:** MS 'Et va trouuer maniere de (*one word illeg.*) une gonnelle rouge a sa fille que vestit et une poullaile roti que mengast.'

54/17 **vysage:** MS 'doulz visage'.

54/24 **by these vestymentes:** *MS* omits. **that I shold ... purpoos:** *MS* omits.
54/25 **that I shold do so:** *MS* omits.
54/26 **& thenne she ... henne:** *MS* 'Et fist semblant de sentir puir la geline.'
54/27 **sone of the duke:** *MS*, *L* 'luy'.
54/30 **She ... henne:** *MS* 'Et la damoiselle print congie delle et dist ...'
54/31 **dame dyane hir moder:** *MS* adds 'Et par raison de la response de vienne en grant desir attendit troys jours pensant que vienne vousist consentir au mariage.'
54/36 **camen:** *MS* adds 'en la prison'.
55/2 **pryson:** *MS* 'en celle maniere'.
55/3 **for hungre:** *MS* omits.
55/13 **playsaunces and lybertees:** *MS* 'franche liberte'.
55/18 **for you:** *MS* 'pour lamour de vous'.
55/22 **how be it ... hert:** *MS* 'mais vous nestes pas celuy a qui mon cuer est octroye'.
55/26 **than I fele:** *MS* is clearer 'que ne sont cestez'.
55/28 **that yf it endure in me:** *MS* omits.
55/31 **& ye shall ... me:** *MS* 'et sentierez ma maladie'.
56/9 **the lyf of vyenne:** literally from the French.
56/12 *MS* begins a new chapter: 'Comment edouard fist fere une chappelle aupres la prison de vienne'.
56/14 **thens:** *MS* 'de prison senon morte'.
56/16ff. Here in *Ver. II* is a much shortened account of Edward's coming to Vienne's prison by way of a tunnel from the chapel he has made. The more detailed account of this occurs earlier in *Ver. I*.
56/29 **fynysshed:** *MS* omits.
57/5–17 Not in *Ver. I*.
57/10 **parlament ... bourgoyne:** *L* 'parlement quelle auoit fait de la geline'.
57/25 *MS* begins a new chapter: 'Comment paris sen ala en terre estrange chercher les pelerinaiges.'
57/28–29 **& almoost was ... sorowe:** *MS* omits.
57/31 **harme ... suffred:** *MS* 'mal que son pere luy faysoit porter'.
57/32 **nyght and day:** *MS* omits.
57/35–58/2 **Alas ... tydynges:** *MS* is somewhat different: 'Pource que ne veulx plus en lieu ou elle puisse auoir nouuelles de moy mais comme personne desperence de toulte consolacion

mondaine men vray tant loing que de moy ne pourra avoir nouvelles ou je seray.'
58/3   **veray god of heuen:** *MS* 'sire dieu'.
58/4   **hyr:** *MS* 'noble vienne'.
58/10 No chapter break in *MS*. Heading in *L* 'Comment paris manda unes lettres a edouard.'
58/21 **fro that contree:** *MS* omits.
58/24 This episode is given in much detail in *Ver. I.* Paris goes first to Venize, then back to Genes, then with Bertrand Picartville to Romanie. Then follows a long letter from Paris to Edward telling of his future plans. **Incontynent:** *MS* omits.
58/30 **dede:** *MS* begins a new chapter 'De Paris qui aprint a parler le maure avant quil entrast en turquie'.
58/30–59/2 **And thenne ... alwaye:** *MS* omits.
59/3   No break in *MS*. *L* 'Comment Paris monta sur mer a venize pour aller au sainct sepulchre en iherusalem.'
59/4   **wyth hys seruaunte:** *MS* omits.
59/5   **where he ... that he:** *MS* omits. **took shyppyng ... cam:** *L* 'ou il monta sur mer et fit tant quil vint'.
59/6   In *Ver. I* he sailed to Constantinople, then to Tauris. He learned the language and even began to look so much like a Moor that no one knew he was French.
59/8   **mounte of caluarye and of Iherusalem:** *MS* 'cayre et des Indes'. In *Sp* 'fueron en Costantinopla que era una grant ciudad de los griegos y aqui Paris pregunto por el camino de Çati y delas Indias ...'.
59/10 **pylgrymage:** *L* omits.
59/11 **moores:** *MS* adds 'et le grec'.
59/12 **mouryske:** *MS* 'ses deulx langaiges'.
59/13 **ynde:** *MS* 'la terre de prestre ihann'. **Ande so ferre ... Iohan:** *MS* omits.
59/13–59/27 Not in *Ver. I*.
59/16 **of a more:** *MS* 'du pays'.
59/21 **sepulture ... sayntuaryes:** *MS* 'les sains lieulx'.
59/28 **Egypte:** *MS* 'babilone'; *L* has 'aultre pt'. Perhaps 'Egypte' is a misreading of 'pt' in the source. Here *Ver. I* shifts the scene back to Europe. Pope Innocent has proclaimed a crusade. Then follows a long account of the assembly of the crusaders from all countries. The King of France is made the leader. When the Dauphin suggests that they send a spy disguised as a pilgrim, they vote that he be the one to go.

102 *Notes*

59/28 **of the soudan:** *MS* omits.
59/29-30 **hyred ... Infortune:** *MS* 'Et la va louer dieu de sa fortune si cruelle et de celle de vienne.'
59/31-32 **whan ... lordes:** *MS* 'quant veoit que sarrasins tenoient celle terre saincte'. **wexe lordes:** *L* 'seignourissoient'.
60/3 **and that fawcon ... other:** *MS* omits.
60/13 **beste:** *MS* omits.
60/15-16 **and bad hym ... dyd:** *MS* 'quil luy en donnast a menger'. *L* and *C* agree: 'collast aux piedz du faulcon'. *MS* seems more logical.
60/18-20 **wherof þe souldan ... courte:** *MS* omits.
60/24-26 *MS* begins a new chapter: 'Du dauphin qui sen alla espier les juseaulz (?) sarrasins & fust prins'.
60/35 **dukes/ Erles ... lordes:** *MS* omits.
61/1 *C, L* agree on heading.
61/7 **also ... our:** *MS* omits.
61/13 **for to espye ... passages:** *L* omits.
61/27 **he sente letters to hys wyf:** *MS* 'manda a madame Dyane sa fame'.
62/1 No break in *MS* and no heading in *L* but a large capital and space.
62/2 **Surrye and damaske** are not in *Ver. I*, which instead lists 'Aigues Mortes' and 'Chippres'.
62/2 **Iherusalem:** *MS* adds a confused statement not in *C* and *L*: 'Touteffoys a la fin luy vausist petit son trauail.'
62/4 **contree:** *MS* adds 'avec les x christiens qui illec estoit'. Then *MS* repeats the line 62/2 'Touteffoys, etc.'
62/6 *Ver. I* contains a long account of Paris's journey, how he cured the sultan's falcons of sickness, and so won his friendship.
62/12 **Ramon:** *MS, Sp, L* 'Rama'; *Ver. I* 'ville pres de Jherusalem'. Perhaps modern Ramallah, a city near Jerusalem to the north.
62/28 ff. *MS* omits the account of the Pope and the King of France trying to ransom the Dauphin. *MS* begins a new chapter with the heading: 'Or laissons le daulphin et retornons a Paris. Comment Paris parla aux deulx cordeliers.'
63/7-9 **These two freres ... them:** *MS* 'Et ses deux freres estoient de la partie de eleuante. Et quant furent en babilloyne il regarderent la cite par maintez pars.' *L* 'Ces deux freres estoient des parties deuers le vent/ lesquelz quand furent en celle partye/ si aduint que en allant par la ville/ paris les trouua.'

Notes 103

63/10 demaunded . . . partyes : *L* 'demanda des parties de parde cha'.
63/18 in the langage of moure : *MS* omits.
63/21 partyes : *L* 'parties deuers le vent'.
63/29 sette . . . passe : *MS* omits.
63/38 good and effecte : *MS* 'a perfection'.
64/14 alwaye . . . moure : *MS* omits.
64/18 by my lawe : *MS* 'par le loy de Mahomet'.
64/26–27 wende . . . aduenture : *MS* omits.
64/29 knowleche : *MS* 'amitie'.
65/24 *MS*, *L* begin a new chapter: *MS* 'Comment Paris alla en alixandre pour veoir le dauphin'; *L* 'Comment paris auec deux freres sen alla en alexandrie et la fut receut de lamiral moult honnorablement'.
65/34 clad : *MS* adds 'auec le grant barbe quil auoit'.
65/37 toure . . . pryson : *MS* 'au millieu de la cite'.
66/4 theste : *MS* 'levant'; *L* 'du vent'. Not in *Ver. I*.
66/23 curtoysly : *MS* adds 'Et le daulphin luy rendit son salut moult gracieusement.'
67/3 of Fraunce : *MS* 'du monde'.
67/6 pryson : *L* 'dillec'.
67/9 frere : *MS* adds : 'que jamais nauoit ouy dire que en ung maure eust tant de bien comme il auoit en celluy que si doulcement le consoloit'; *L* 'cellui qui le confortoit/ que pechie estoit quil nestoit crestien'.
67/16 In *Ver. I* the scene shifts to Vienne and tells of a dream she has had in prison, that an eagle came and led her outside. be welcome : *L*, *MS* omit.
67/21 & in caas . . . secretely : *MS* 'et en cas que vous y ayes vollente essaiez le mais quil se puisse faire secretement'.
67/26 that he . . . : *MS* 'quil me jure quil me . . .'
68/3 god bare hym awaye : *MS* 'il luy sembloit que nostre seigneur luy estoit apparu'. thanke god & : *MS* and *L* omit 'god &'.
68/8 In *Ver. I* he swears that he will give him his daughter as his wife.
68/26–69/32: not in *MS*.
68/33 but . . . porte : *L* 'mais que pour le port on luy baillast la moytie de largent'.
68/37 shal come : *L* adds 'pour moy recueillir'.
68/38 lodgyng : *L* adds 'avec le freres'.

69/2 **prouysyon ... towellys:** L 'daultres prouisions de mantilz et touailles'.

69/4 L starts a new chapter with heading: 'Comment paris deliura le daulphin de prison en alexandrie.' **Whan ... sayd:** L 'Quand cecy fut faict sur le tard si dist paris aux gardes de la prison.'

69/17 **yates:** not in L.

69/24 L begins new chapter with heading: 'Comment le daulphin et paris sen retournerent par mer.'

69/28 **place:** L adds 'en leuant'; 'Baruth' in MS and Sp, but this sentence follows the statement that he borrowed money.

69/29 **wente a londe:** L 'descendit'.

70/16 MS and L begin a new chapter. MS 'Comment chevaliers du dauphine vindrent au deuant du dauphin'; L 'Comment le daulphin et Paris furent receus du peuple de france en grand ioye & en grand honneur'.

70/24 **that noo man ... it:** MS omits.

70/27 **reuerence & honour:** MS 'honneur'.

70/32 In *Ver. I* the dauphin does the explaining and at length.

70/36 **londe:** MS begins a new chapter here with no heading except the word 'Paris' written between. MS ff. 52^r and 52^v are not represented in C. They read: 'Apres aucuns jours que la feste fust passee Paris estoit moult angoisseulx en son couraige pensant en son couraige en quelle maniere pourroit veoir Vienne Et ainssy comme amours le chasserient nuyt et jour sen alla a lostel des freres cordilliers Et Paris tira apart celluy qui sauoit parler le maure Et luy dist seigneur vous sauez bien que deuant que le dauphin saillist de prison il me jura deuant vous quil me donneroit toult ce quil que je luy demanderoye Et ne dist pas que me tienge pour content de ce quil me fait Touteffoys sil luy plaisoit de me faire une grace je luy en sauvoye plus de gre que sil me donnoit toute sa terre Et la grace que luy vueil demander est ceste Quil me donne sa fille pour fame quil a tenue si longuement en prison Et pource je vous prie que vous y aillez et luy dictes Et si par auenture luy desplaisoit pour ce que je suis maure dictes luy que je me feray christien Et le frere voyant que Paris disoit verite de ce que le dauphin luy avoit promis dist que par sa foy il ferait son pouoir Et incontinent le frere sen alla au dauphin sans aultre et luy dist toult le fait Et lors le dauphin dist sans aultre accort que bien luy plaisoit quil eust sa fille Mais il se doubtoit quelle ne vousist pas fort Pource que jamais nauoit voullu prendre mari

Touteffoys esseyons le Et incontinent le frere sans partir dillec et sen alla a paris Et luy va dire et conter la responce que le dauphin luy avoit faicte De la quelle Paris fust moult joyeulx en son cuer Et le dauphin ordonna que levesque de saint lorens et le frere deussent lendemain aller parler de ce fait a Vienne Et il allerent Et quant furent deuant Vienne le frere cordelier parla primement et dist.'

71/6 **moure**: *L* 'dieu et le moure'.

71/8 **fader**: *MS* adds 'et vous contessiez quil est de grant lignaige et moult saige homme'.

71/14 **sayeng**: *MS* adds 'seigneurs je croy bien que toult ce que dictes est vray'.

71/25 **the moure**: *MS* 'Paris'. **& so . . . parys**: *MS* omits and adds 'et Paris voyant quil nauoit riens peu achever est hausse de lamour de Vienne envoya au dauphyn sil luy plaisoit quil allast parler a elle Et le dauphin dist que bien luy plaisoit'.

72/1–3 **and therfor . . . honour**: *MS* 'et pource vous prie que vous la fariez'.

72/3 **And yet more . . . not**: *MS* 'car aussi deuez vous obeir au commandement de vostre pere'.

72/21–22 **moche good of you . . . my fader**: *MS* 'que bien appart que vous estes celuy que lon dist'.

72/27 **vyenne . . . two quarters**: *MS* 'Et Vienne auoit fait la mediecine quelle auoit fait au duc de bourgoigne des quartiers . . .'

72/32 **they**: *MS* 'Vienne'.

73/25 *MS*, *L* begin a new chapter: *MS* 'Comment paris retourna a vienne auec le cordelier'; *L* 'Comment paris vint veoir vienne en la prison et comment elle le recongneut'.

73/27 **ryche swerde**: *MS* 'espee moresque'.

73/31 **auowed**: *MS* adds 'a dieu'.

74/3 **sorowe & payne**: *MS* 'ceste vie douloureuse'.

74/9 **by cause . . . ageyn**: *MS* omits.

74/14 **wente oute**: *MS*, *L* 'eslongea de la prison (*MS* maison)'.

75/10 **& she . . . alle**: *MS* omits.

75/11 **she had watched**: *MS* 'car la nuyt de deuant auoit este ennuye . . .'

75/12 **nyght byfore**: *MS*, *L* add 'et ainsi estoit fort endormie'.

76/10 *C*, *L* omit a passage in *MS*: 'Et lors paris tira son espee moresque quil portoit sainturet Et la penit par la pointe Et se mist agenoulx devant le dauphin Et dist telles parolles Moult puissant et hault seigneur plaise vous de moy pardonner pource que jay mallement failli envers vous Touteffoys monseigneur ne suige pas le premier qui ayt defailli Car les plus saiges du monde y ont failly Et aussi monseigneur veez cy Paris vostre indigne vaisal et subjet fils a missir jacques. Et puis quil a pleu a mon seigneur que je soye venu en ceste aventure je demande vostre misericorde Touteffoys mon seigneur si vous veez que plus grand soit le desplaisir que le plaisir que vous ay fait veez vous cy mon espee et prenes de mon corps dela ou vous plaira vengeance Quant le sires du dauphin ouyrent ainsy parler le maure Et puis daultre part quil disoit quil estoit Paris il demouverent toulx esbahis Et parce espalir le dauphin car si souvent lauoit veu a sa court et ne lauoit cogneu.'

76/18–21 **And also . . . Ioyous**: *L* omits.

76/26 **and after this . . . doulphyn**: *L* 'et quand eut ce mene ung petit il dit au daulphin'.

76/29 In *Ver. I* Edward and Paris's father and mother are present at the castle.

77/4 Chapter heading in *L*: 'Comment paris espousa vienne et de la feste qui y fut faicte.'

77/14 **world**: *MS, L* add 'Et croy que leur aduenture fut mieulx de dieu que de nulle aultre personne.'

77/15 *Ver. I* 'sept enfans quatre filz et troys filhes'.

77/26 *Ver. I* says Paris died aged 105 and Vienne five years later, aged 97.

77/31–78/4 Not in *MS. L* ends with the colophon: 'cy finist listoire du vaillant et noble cheualier paris Et de la belle vienne fille du daulphin de viennois Emprientee en Anuers par moy Gherard leeu. lan Mil CCCC lxxxvii.le.xv^e. iour du mois de May'.

GLOSSARY

a *conj.* and 7/30.
abasshe *refl. v.* be cast down 53/10.
absente *refl. v.* absent oneself, keep away 33/28.
abyden *pp.* waited 53/19.
abylemens *n. pl.* furnishings, trappings 22/3.
accesse *n.* attack of fever 21/10.
accomplisshed *pp.* ended 38/17.
accorde *n.* agreement 3/17.
accorded *pp.* arranged 50/6.
accordyng (to) *pr. p.* proper (to) 12/37.
achyeued *pp.* completed 56/29.
admerueylled *pp. adj.* astonished 67/19.
admonested *v.* admonished 52/2.
admyral *n.* an emir or officer under a sultan 65/28.
adresse *v.* prepare 34/30.
aduenture *n.* fortune, lot 45/13, 45/19; in what ∼ I am dysposed in what plight I am placed 56/2.
aduyse *v.* inform 27/14; consider 25/21; spy out 62/3.
aferde *adj.* afraid 39/7.
afore *adv.* before 4/6; *prep.* 1/14.
after *prep.* according to 1/21; *adv.* afterwards 2/2.
agaynsayest *v.* contradictest 23/33.
ageyn *adv.* back 35/18.
ageynst, ayenst *prep.* for 72/8; against 8/8; towards 20/14.
agreable *adj. in phr.* haue . . . ∼ consent to 51/6.
agryeued *pp. adj.* angered 58/23.
all day *adv.* every day, daily 22/23.
alle *adv.* wholly 33/4.
allonge *adv.* entirely, from beginning to end 47/35.
allowed *pp.* praised 14/12.
a londe *adv.* ashore 69/29.
also . . . as as . . . as 53/27.
alwaye *adv.* at all events 8/4.
amended *v.* recovered (from sickness) 60/17.
amerous *adj.* beloved 7/31.

ameruaylled *pp.* struck with wonder or amazement 7/7.
amorouste *n.* love 3/2.
amytye *n.* friendship 19/36.
anguysshous *adj.* causing distress 46/6.
annoyed *pp.* disturbed, troubled 69/30.
apparaylle *n.* preparation 12/16.
apparaylled *pp. adj.* prepared 61/14.
appeased *v.* quieted 40/24.
apperceyue *v.* perceive, observe 61/17.
apperteyneth *v.* is fitting 14/7.
appertyse *n.* dexterity, skill (in arms) 2/33.
arayed *pp.* vanquished, routed 5/18; arrayed 7/6.
armes *n. pl.* armorial bearings 8/3; equipment including armour 5/11; do ∼ perform warlike exploits 20/30.
Armynak Armagnac 14/27.
assaye *v.* attempt 31/3.
assemble *n.* assembly, gathering 6/30.
assemble *v.* join 50/33.
atte at the 11/26.
aualed *pp.* subsided 37/2.
auowed *pp.* vowed, declared 51/16.
auoyded *v.* departed 22/30.
ayenst *see* ageynst.
Aygues mortes Aigues-Mortes, an old Roman town on the Rhône delta, once accessible to the Mediterranean by canal. In the Middle Ages it was an important Mediterranean port 35/7.

babylone Babylon, often in the Middle Ages used loosely for the Near East 62/7.
bauyers Bavaria 14/26.
be *pp.* been 9/27.
beale, bele *adj.* beautiful 46/9, 47/17.
beaulte *n.* beauty 1/12.
become, bycomen *pp.* gone 9/7, 36/30.
befyl *v.* came about 10/31.
benedyctyon *n.* blessing 45/29.

Glossary

bere oute v. confirm 12/9; **bare oute** pt. supported 9/16, 10/36.
besaunts n. pl. bezants, gold coins issued at Byzantium; they had a wide circulation in Europe from c. 800 to the middle of the thirteenth century. 68/31.
betymes adv. at an early hour 73/25.
borowe v. be surety for 76/27.
bounte n. valour 19/13.
bowclers n. pl. small hand shields 5/12.
braband Brabant 20/29.
brake v. made known 3/12.
brennyng pr. p. burning 3/7.
brethern n. pl. brothers 2/31.
broched v. spurred 8/17.
bruyt n. fame 9/24.
by prep. through 4/33; on 59/13.
by cause conj. so that 69/22.
bycomen see **become**.
byleue n. belief 59/18.

caas n. condition 29/17; **in ~ that** conj. in the event that 67/21.
canstyke n. candlestick 23/3.
Carnes 6/29. The Fr. has *Tanes*; I have not been able to identify either.
cartayn see **certeyn**.
caytyf adj. miserable 57/36.
certefye v. assure 48/19.
certeyn adv. certainly 3/24; **for cartayn** for certain 35/3.
certes adv. certainly 19/16.
chaas v. chose 36/23.
chapelet n. chaplet, garland 28/29.
charge n. duty 40/28.
charged pp. burdened 26/33.
chargeable adj. in phr. **vnto hym ~ his** responsibility 43/15.
chere n. face, countenance 26/13; reception, entertainment 9/10.
chyualrye n. body of knights 50/22; usages of knighthood 46/5; pl. deeds of chivalry 14/9.
clene adj. skilful 2/24.
cleped pp. named 1/11.
cloos adj. closed 25/26.
coler, colyer n. a chain or band worn by knights as an ornament or sign of identification 11/35, 24/30.

concluded v. determined, decided 53/23.
condycyons n. pl. conduct 24/5.
conne v. be able 55/14.
constrayned v. compelled 6/33.
consydered pp. being taken into account 39/20 (an absolute participle construction; cf. Fr. *considéré que*).
contente see **euyl**.
coped v. fought 15/15.
cordable adj. agreeable 3/9.
cornes n. pl. ? corners 13/15 (emended to corners).
couerture n. cover, trappings 22/18.
countenaunces n. pl. (with **make**) comport oneself 40/12, 45/8; **made a countenaunce** made a show 21/4.
courage n. thought, intent, heart 5/36, 53/29, 59/23.
courrour n. courier 47/3.
crased pp. adj. ill 22/26.
croysee n. crusade 62/17.
crystyente n. Christendom 60/32.
curtoys adj. courteous 41/33.
custommes n. pl. customs 2/15.

dalphyne Dauphiné 17/26.
damage, dommage n. pity 56/6, 74/2.
damaske Damascus 62/2.
damoysel n. lady in waiting 4/8.
daulphyn n. a feudal title in France borne first by lords of Vienne and Auvergne and later by the eldest son of the king. It was first used in the early part of the twelfth century, but was not generally recognized as a title until the latter part of the thirteenth century. No dauphin of Vienne bore the name of Geoffrey d'Alenson. 1/3; **dolphyn** 19/23; **doulphyn** 21/29.
deffaulte n. default, defection 56/13; fault, neglect 55/4.
deffende v. forbid 30/33; defend 5/13.
deme(a)ned v. behaved, conducted 2/16; expressed 75/13.
departyng vbl. n. departure 33/33.
deposed pp. deprived 45/22.
derke adj. dark 53/1.
derly adv. earnestly 20/37.
despayred pp. adj. in despair 40/5.
desplaysyr see **dysplaysyr**.

Glossary 109

destrayned v. disturbed, compelled 25/3, 26/25.
deuoyr n. duty 32/8.
deye v. die 31/38; deyeden pt. pl. 77/21.
do, doo v. auxil. cause, have 7/5, 33/15; doon, doo pp. done 24/16, 31/14.
dolant adj. sad 19/14.
dommage see damage.
doubted v. feared 40/5.
doubtous adj. questionable 31/24.
doubtyng pr. p. fearing 24/17.
doulphyne n. dauphinate 72/1.
drede n. fear 64/4.
duelleden v. lived 21/9.
duresse n. hardness, firmness 55/6.
dygne adj. worthy 1/12.
dyscomforted pp. disconcerted 23/32.
dyscouerd pp. revealed 26/3.
dysease n. discomfort 48/17.
dysobeyssaunt adj. disobedient 5/8.
dysplaysyr, desplaysyr n. distress, unhappiness 4/33, 25/10.
dysporte n. pleasure 2/25.

effecte n. fulfilment 63/38.
eft ones adv. again 61/23.
egal adj. equal 23/26.
emong(e) prep. among 2/10.
emprysed pp. adj. undertaken 35/33.
enchaunted pp. adj. in ~ werke witchcraft 74/33.
encreaced v. increased 53/8.
endured pp. lasted 48/3.
enforce v. encourage 29/18; refl. strive 22/24.
enformed refl. v. learned 59/7.
enpayreth v. impairs 71/21.
ensaumple n. example 62/21.
ensure v. assure 28/3.
entendement n. mind, spirit 12/8, 19/15; intention 45/23.
entencion n. fixed design 42/17.
enterprysed pp. undertaken 29/10.
enuyronned pp. surrounded 11/36.
eschaunge n. bill of exchange 48/31.
eschewe v. avoid 39/16.
especyal in phr. in ~ especially 42/13.
esprysed pp. inflamed 3/7.
espye v. spy out 5/25.

estate n. situation 56/19; condition 23/27.
estraunge v. separate 58/21.
eueryche pron. each one 14/5.
euyl adv. ill; ~ contente, ~ dysposed ill-disposed 20/13, 51/14; adj. evil 65/2; ~ wylle ill-will 45/28.
excusacyon n. excuse 51/14.
extymacyon n. value 11/34.
eyther (of them) pron. every one (of them) 12/7.

fantasye n. fancy 8/4.
fauce porte n. secret door, postern 36/1.
faute n. in phr. wythoute ~ without fail, for a certainty 27/15; faulte fault, error 39/18.
fayte, feat n. deed, event 2/19, 38/12.
felawshyp n. company 10/9.
fele v. undergo 55/26; felte pp. perceived (of smell) 55/37.
felonnye n. anger 32/24, 33/24.
felowe n. companion, friend 6/34; see preuy ~ , secrete ~ .
ferre adv. far 23/21.
feste v. regale, sumptuously entertain 50/17.
fette v. fetched 38/22.
fewtred v. put into the fewter or rest 17/9.
flouryng pr. p. in phr. ~ age bloom of youth, prime of life 3/6.
floyted v. played on a flute 76/13.
folyly adv. foolishly 55/3.
for prep. with, on account of 12/34, 25/27; ~ cause that because 12/24; ~ thys that because 6/2.
force n. need 40/23.
forthon in phr. fro thenne ~ from then onwards 57/15, 58/17.
foteman n. soldier not mounted 40/25.
foundement n. foundation 56/26.
fowles n. pl. birds 22/5.
free adj. noble 39/1; ~ knyght one not attached to any lord 15/33.
fro prep. from 4/26; ~ hym self beside himself, out of his senses 31/36; fro ... to from .. to 35/11.
from prep. of 5/11.
furnysshe v. complete 16/23.

Glossary

fuste *n.* a light galley usually with sixteen oars to a side and a light sail, a foist 68/28.
fyl *v.* fell 15/29.
fylled *pp.* satiated 26/14.
fynaunces *n. pl.* bribes, offers of money 62/30.

gaf *see* **gyueth.**
gate *v.* got, won 7/17 (*heading*).
Gene, Genes Genoa 40/11, 45/21.
gentylnes *n.* good breeding 1/15.
ghoostly *adj.* spiritual 27/8.
graunted *v.* agreed 12/36.
greued *pp.* discomforted, afflicted 69/30.
grounde *n.* floor 23/15.
growed *v.* grew 3/6.
gryef *n.* hurt, harm 42/17.
guyse *n.* custom 7/9.
gyueth *v.* suggests 9/33 (N.E.D. *give v.* VI, 22); **gaf oute a croysee** proclaimed a crusade 60/29.

habylled *pp. adj.* clothed, armed 14/29.
happed *impers. v.* came about 2/8.
harde *adj.* brave 52/9; **hardy** 11/1.
hardly *adv.* severely 32/26.
hardynes *n.* bravery 2/27.
harneysed *v.* equipped 6/38.
harnoys *n.* armour 6/37.
hauoyr *n.* property 1/6.
henge *v.* hung 22/36.
henne *n.* hen 54/24.
hert *n.* heart 45/6; mind, purpose 7/12.
herytage *n.* property to be inherited 45/33.
herytyer *n.* inheritor 77/18.
heuy *adj.* sorrowful 45/3.
holden *pp. in phr.* **be ~ to** to be obliged, under obligation to 28/37; **holdeth ... on** depends on 54/1.
hole *adj.* in health 60/8; **hool** 24/35.
holpen *pp.* helped 71/35.
holy sepulture the Holy Sepulchre 59/21.
honestly *adv.* appropriately 26/30.
hon(n)este *adj.* fitting, appropriate to persons of standing, honourable 19/33, 55/29.
horsed *pp.* mounted on horses 7/21.

hostry *n.* hostel 64/10.
hye *adj.* noble 55/24.
hyely *adv.* nobly 33/13.
hyght *v.* was called, named 2/30.

Iape *n.* deception 37/24.
Iayler *n.* gaoler 52/32.
Incontynent *adv.* immediately 11/4.
Indigne *adj.* unworthy 29/21.
Indurate *adj.* obdurate 52/12.
Infortune *n.* misfortune 59/30.
in soo moche that to such a degree that 1/7, 2/21.
Iourneye *n.* day 17/32.
Ioustes *n. pl.* (as *sg.*) tournament 11/17.
Ioyaulx *n. pl.* jewels 13/27.
Ioyouste *n.* joy 29/33.

kepest *v.* payest attention to 32/27.
kerued *v.* carved 7/16.
knowleche *n.* recognition 70/30.
knowyng *vbl. n.* knowledge 76/18.
kynrede *n.* kindred 1/4.

ladyes maydens *n. pl.* young ladies 13/34.
ladyshyp *n. in phr.* **your ~** translates Fr. *madame* 28/2.
large *adj. in phr.* **at ~** copiously 47/15.
late *v.* let 55/25.
leef *adj. in phr.* **had as ~ to** would as soon 40/22.
lenger *compar. adv.* longer 44/1.
lepen *v.* leapt 36/1.
lerned *v.* taught 6/1
lese *v.* lose 10/24.
leuer *compar. adv.* rather 4/35.
leuyng *vbl. n.* omission 29/7.
loenge *n.* praise 8/28.
longe *see* **thought.**
loo *interj.* lo! 39/29.
lordes *n. pl. in phr.* **wexe ~** become noblemen (Fr. *seignourissoient*) 59/32.
lordshyppe *n.* domain of a lord (Fr. *aultre terre*) 34/21.
loue *n.* loved one 47/18.
loued *v.* praised 9/16.
loyally *adv.* legally 16/13.
lyf *n.* health, condition, 56/9.
lyghtly *adv.* quickly 36/17.

Glossary

lykly *adj.* likely, probable 3/9.
lystes *n. pl.* barriers enclosing a field for a tournament 6/5.
lyuerey *n.* device 12/10.

made *pp. in phr.* ~ **of** esteemed 1/7.
mageste *n. in phr.* ~ **of our lord the Host** 23/2.
maner *n.* manner (of) 3/33.
mantellys *n. pl.* mantles, cloaks 69/2.
matrymonye *n.* marriage 77/16.
maundement *n.* command 11/18.
mayntene *v.* support, defend in tournament 13/34.
menace *v.* threaten 42/21.
menaces *n. pl.* threats 52/3.
menchon *n.* nun 33/12.
mencyon *n.* mention, *or perhaps here*, praise 22/16.
meschaunt *adj.* miserable 20/7.
mesprysed *pp.* misbehaved 41/18.
mestyer *n.* occupation 67/30.
mete *n.* food 40/7.
moche *adv.* very 19/15.
moeued *v.* stirred up 9/13.
mondayne *adj.* worldly 45/23.
moo *compar. adj.* more 16/37.
moost *adj.* greatest 6/19.
morne *n.* morning; **on the** ~ **at nyght** the night of the next day, the next evening 36/8. *See to* ~.
moure *n.* Moor 63/20; **langage of** ~ language of the Moors 63/19.
mouryske, mourysshe *n.* language of the Moors 59/12, 66/12.
mowe *v.* be able 54/11.
moyen *n.* means 19/16.
mustre *v.* pass in review 7/25; **mostred** *pt.* 7/26.
myrthe *n.* pleasure through music 3/18.
myscreauntes *n. pl.* unbelievers, infidels 60/30.

naked *adj.* unarmed 5/11.
ne *adv.* nor 10/25, 18/7; *expletive* 68/11.
neuew *n.* nephew 6/26.
noblesse *n.* noble company 15/9.
nothyng *adv.* not at all (*with adj.*) 53/15.
nourysshed *pp.* brought up 1/27.

of *prep.* on account of 26/11; by 1/8; with 6/37.
one *num.* one, the same 2/31; ~ **so** such a 39/10.
onely *adj.* single 29/7.
ones *adv.* once 16/18.
or *conj.* before 4/34; ~ **that** *conj.* 33/11.
ordeyne *v.* provide 21/32; plan, devise 45/13.
ordure *n.* filth 31/3.
ordynaunce *n.* display 13/18.
orysons *n. pl.* prayers 25/20.
other *pron.* others 2/28, 59/31.
ouerthrewe *v.* fell 16/5.
ouerlonge *adj.* tedious 13/30.
outher *adv.* either 4/12; other 4/19.

pacyence *n. in phr.* **take in** ~ accept with resignation 67/5.
pareylle *adj.* equal 41/23.
pariured *pp.* perjured 72/18.
parlament *n.* speech 30/10.
parte *n. in phr.* on that other ~ on the other hand 57/30.
parte *v.* share 34/25.
party *n.* predicament 4/32.
partye *n.* part 44/37.
partyes *n. pl.* countries 63/21.
passages *n. pl.* stations along the way 35/17.
passed *pp. adj.* gone by, ago 20/29.
passyng *adv.* exceedingly 32/13.
patrone *n.* master of a galley or ship 68/30.
peased *pp.* appeased, pacified 34/9.
pensyf *adj.* pensive 57/32.
pensyful *adj.* thoughtful 6/2.
perdurable *adj.* everlasting 77/30.
persones *n. pl.* physical power 13/33.
peryl *n.* ? peril 46/2.
peryllous *adj.* dangerous 15/20.
playsaunces *n. pl.* pleasures 55/13.
playsaunt *adj.* pleasing 1/19.
pleseth *v.* may it please 25/8; **plased** *pt.* pleased 26/21.
poursyewed *pp.* attended, followed 46/2.
pourueyed *v.* provided 6/37.
poynte *n.* predicament 62/15.
praye *v.* ask 28/20.

Glossary

prees *n.* crowd 13/15.
presentacyon *n.* offering 49/11.
prester Iohan Prester John 59/14.
preuy felowe *n.* confidant 4/8.
procedyng *in phr.* ~ **your degree** surpassing you in station or position 12/28.
pronounced *pp.* announced 6/18.
prouffyt *n.* profit 51/8.
prys *n.* esteem 8/26.
pryuely *adv.* secretly 4/18.
pryuete *n.* private affairs or counsel 31/29.
pucelle *n.* young girl 7/31.
punycyon *n.* punishment 58/9.
puyssaunce *n.* strength 63/7.
puyssauntly *adv.* powerfully 15/19.
pyght *pp.* set 13/14.
pyned *pp.* tortured 62/14.

quarelle *n.* dispute, contention 12/13.
quasi *adv.* as it were, virtually 25/23, 31/12.
quyck *adj.* alive 37/17.

Ramon Ramallah, a city near Jerusalem 62/12.
rebuked *pp.* treated lightly 12/36.
recountred *v.* encountered 8/9.
recourders *n. pl.* recorders, flutes 3/20.
redoubted *adj.* reverenced 32/11.
regarde *n.* respect 72/7; *in phr.* **nouȝt to the** ~ not at all like 4/9.
reherce *v.* recount 22/7.
renne *v.* run 73/1.
renom(m)ee *n.* renown 2/5, 2/21.
replenysshed *pp.* filled 1/15.
repreuyng *pr. p.* reproving 42/5.
requyred *pp.* sought 30/20.
resplendysshed *v.* sparkled 13/28.
retche *v.* reckon 58/18.
reuerence *n. in phr.* **do the** ~ **to make obeisance to** 26/6.
rote *n.* bottom (of heart) 9/36.
royame *n.* realm 1/10.
ryal *adj.* royal 9/10.
ryȝt *adv.* very 1/5, 42/2.
ryuen *pp.* thrust 38/36.

sacrefyse *n.* offering of prayer 23/4.
sacyat *pp. adj.* satiated 47/12.
salewed *v.* greeted, 4/27, 21/19.
sauf *prep.* except 3/11, 26/3.
sayntuaryes *n. pl.* sanctuaries, holy places 59/21.
scaffold *n.* a gallery for spectators 7/5.
seche *v.* seek 40/25.
secrete felowe confidant 19/35.
seek, seke *adj.* sick 21/8 (*heading*), 21/16.
seen *pp.* seeing, considering (*cf.* Fr. vu) 41/21; similarly **seyng** *pr. p.* 52/11.
semblable *adj.* similar 22/23 (**semalable** C), 41/25.
semblaunte *n.* sign 10/10, 42/3; **semblaunter** (*presumably erroneous form*) 63/37.
sentence *n.* judgment 11/13.
sepulture *see* **holy.**
serd 60/19 (*emended to* **lord**).
sette by held in high esteem 12/27.
shamefastnes *n.* modesty 51/19.
sheweth *v. intr.* appears 1/14.
shortely *adv.* soon 34/27.
shyppyng *n. in phr.* **took** ~ embarked 59/5.
shytte *v.* shut 22/30.
slee *v.* slay 23/37.
slode *v.* slipped 16/5.
songe *v.* sang 76/13.
souerayn *adj.* supreme 75/35.
soulas *n.* delight, joy 75/28.
souldan *n.* sultan 62/7.
soupe *v.* dine 69/8.
sowne *n.* sound 3/28.
sowned *v.* made music 4/7.
space *n.* time, opportunity 24/3, 42/36.
spack *v.* spoke 75/28.
sparkles *n. pl.* sparks 10/5.
stenche *n.* smell 72/29.
sterops *n. pl.* stirrups 8/12.
stert *v.* started 11/5.
stonken *v.* stank 54/34.
strake *v.* struck 17/11.
strongely *adv.* intently 74/16.
stynche *n.* smell 72/30.
stynte *v.* stop 24/22.
subget *n.* subject 23/30.
submysed *pp.* made subject to 29/24.

Glossary 113

supplye *v.* supplicate 29/14.
supposed *v.* expected 37/13, 58/26.
sure *adj.* safe 36/37.
surely *adv.* safely 34/22.
Surrye Syria 62/2.
swelte *v.* faint 57/9.
syn *conj.* since 10/19; *adv.* afterwards 7/20.
syngars *n. pl.* singers 7/10.
sythe(n) *conj.* since 16/1, 28/11.

tadresse *v.* to prepare 34/30.
taken *pp. adj.* appointed (hour) 35/34; ill, seized with (mental) pain 22/27.
talent *n.* wish 6/15.
terme *n. in phr.* **took ~** (Fr. *prisent terme*) made an appointment 30/4.
thankynges *n. pl.* thanks 18/34.
that *conj.* in order that 3/11.
that one ... that other *phr.* the one ... the other 53/17, 67/12.
the *pron.* thee 19/32.
thembusshement *n.* the ambush 4/22.
them self *pron.* themselves 3/17.
thentendement *n.* the view 77/25.
there as *conj.* where 2/32.
the whiche *rel. pron.* who 2/11.
tho *pron.* those 4/4.
thordynaunce *n.* the arrangement, display 22/16.
thought *n.* anxiety 43/2, 56/17.
thought *v.* seemed 36/23; **~ longe or** grew impatient (for his return) 24/33.
thwonge *n.* thong 22/36.
thycke *adj.* crowded 16/35.
thyder as *conj.* where 4/26.
thynobedyence *n.* the disobedience 55/8.
thystorye *n.* the story 63/1.
to *prep.* as 55/10; in 2/9; for 1/10.
tofore *prep.* before 3/17 (*heading*); **~ or** *conj.* 25/19; **~ that** *conj.* 45/26.
to morne *n.* tomorrow 27/13.
tormented *pp.* tortured 62/14.
torne *v.* turn 36/32.
to thende that so that 18/11.
tourchemen *n. pl.* interpreters 66/14 (N.E.D. *Truchman*).
toward *prep.* to 11/12.
trauaylled *v.* tormented 51/19.

trayted *v.* treated 44/13; negotiated 30/19.
traytre *n.* traitor 42/13.
trayty *n. in phr.* **in ~** under discussion, in treaty 45/3.
treat *v.* negotiate 30/19, 49/5.
trespaced *pp.* committed wrong 41/25.
treylle *n.* window grating 54/37.
truffes *n. pl.* trifles 30/12.
truste *v. in phr.* **Neuer ~ me** you will never believe me 9/30.
tryste *adj.* sad 6/2.
trystesse *n.* sadness 10/9.
tweyne *adj.* two (*in phr.* **bathe ~**) 77/27.
tyerce *n.* tierce, 9 a.m. 15/12.

vnconnyng *adj.* ignorant 49/22.
vnfeter *v.* remove the fetters from 69/16.
vnnethe *adv.* hardly 30/22.
vpon *prep.* of 8/16.

valewe *n.* value 28/8.
valure *n.* value, worth 6/12 (**valurr** C), 22/17; **valoyr** might 16/28.
veray *adj.* true 16/32; *in phr.* **a ~ god** 23/32, 58/3 *it translates* Fr. *vrai dieu*.
vertuous *adj.* valorous 39/7.
vesture *n.* clothing 75/1.
voyde *v.* depart 5/15.
vysage *n.* face 26/20.
vysytacyon *n.* visit (to a sick person) 27/33.
vysyted *pp.* examined 22/34.

wanne *v.* won 28/27.
watched *pp.* lain awake 75/12.
wel *adv.* entirely, very 1/12, 42/32.
wele *n.* good 20/18.
wene *v.* think 54/23.
were *v.* wear 75/1.
westmestre Westminster 78/1.
wete, wyte *v.* know 2/34, 37/33; **that is to ~** (Fr. *cestasavoir*) that is to say, namely 3/4, 14/25; **wyst** *pt.* knew 15/23.
wexe lordes *see* **lordes.**
where as *conj.* where 3/21.
wherfore *conj.* on account of which 68/6.
who *indef. pron.* whosoever 26/19.
whyche *rel. pron.* who 44/15.

whyle (of tyme) *n.* space (of time), a little while 70/31.
whylere *adv.* formerly 9/35.
wonde vp *v.* hoisted 69/26.
woned *pp.* accustomed 19/28.
worshyp *n.* honour 8/15.
wote *v.* know 18/33, 21/27.
wryton *pp.* announced by writing 60/34.
wyces *n. pl.* voices 3/28.
wylle *n.* desire 53/8; *in phr.* **be in ∼ be willing** 67/22.
wyst, wyte *see* **wete.**
wyth *prep.* by 1/28.

wytyngly *adv.* wittingly, consciously 39/2.

yates *n. pl.* gates 69/17.
ye *pron.* you *(singular)* 5/1.
yede *v.* went 3/20.
yeftes *n. pl.* gifts 42/4.
yere *n. pl.* years 2/2.
yeuen *pp.* given 9/31.
ymagynatyf *adj.* thoughtful 40/14.
yongthe *n.* youth 10/26.
ys *adv.* as 66/27 (? *error for* **as**; *cf.* 66/17, 67/32 *etc.*).
yssued *v.* went 42/28.

The manufacturer's authorised representative in the EU for product safety is Oxford University Press España S.A. of El Parque Empresarial San Fernando de Henares, Avenida de Castilla, 2 - 28830 Madrid (www.oup.es/en or product.safety@oup.com). OUP España S.A. also acts as importer into Spain of products made by the manufacturer.

Printed and bound by CPI Group (UK) Ltd, Croydon, CR0 4YY